YEAR C

LISTENING TO GOD'S WORD

Activities and Stories

Eileen Drilling • Judy Rothfork

LTP
LITURGY
TRAINING
PUBLICATIONS

ACKNOWLEDGMENTS

Excerpts from scripture are from the *Contemporary English Version* of the New Testament, Roman Catholic Edition, copyright © 1991, American Bible Society. Reprinted with permission. All rights reserved.

The English translation of the Apostles' Creed by the International Consultation on English texts (ICET). All rights reserved.

Copyright © 1997, Archdiocese of Chicago: Liturgy Training Publications, 1800 North Hermitage Avenue, Chicago IL 60622-1101; 1-800-933-1800; fax 1-800-933-7094; e-mail orders@ltp.org. All rights reserved.

This book was edited by Victoria M. Tufano. Deborah Bogaert was the production editor, with additional assistance from Theresa Houston. Anna Manhart designed the book and illustrated the art on the inside pages. Kari Nicholls was the production artist who typeset the book in Cushing, Officina Sans and Univers. The cover art was drawn by Annika Nelson and colorized by Kristyn Kalnes. Printed by BookCrafters of Chelsea, Michigan.

ISBN 1-56854-209-7
LCATC

Contents

Introduction • iv

Advent • 1
First Sunday of Advent   2
Second Sunday of Advent   5
Third Sunday of Advent   8
Fourth Sunday of Advent   10

Christmas Season • 12
Christmas   13
Holy Family   14
Mary, Mother of God   17
Epiphany   19
Baptism of the Lord   22

Lent • 25
First Sunday of Lent   26
Second Sunday of Lent   30
Third Sunday of Lent   34
Fourth Sunday of Lent   36
Fifth Sunday of Lent   39
Passion (Palm) Sunday   42

Triduum • 44
Holy Thursday   45
Good Friday   46
Holy Saturday   49

Easter Season • 50
Easter   51
Second Sunday of Easter   53
Third Sunday of Easter   56
Fourth Sunday of Easter   58
Fifth Sunday of Easter   60
Sixth Sunday of Easter   62
Seventh Sunday of Easter   64
Pentecost   66

Ordinary Time • 68
Trinity Sunday   69
Body and Blood of Christ   71
Second Sunday   74
Third Sunday   76
Fourth Sunday   79
Fifth Sunday   81
Sixth Sunday   83
Seventh Sunday   86
Eighth Sunday   88
Ninth Sunday   90
Tenth Sunday   92
Eleventh Sunday   94
Twelfth Sunday   97
Thirteenth Sunday   99
Fourteenth Sunday   101
Fifteenth Sunday   103
Sixteenth Sunday   105
Seventeenth Sunday   106
Eighteenth Sunday   108
Nineteenth Sunday   110
Twentieth Sunday   113
Twenty-first Sunday   115
Twenty-second Sunday   117
Twenty-third Sunday   119
Twenty-fourth Sunday   121
Twenty-fifth Sunday   123
Twenty-sixth Sunday   125
Twenty-seventh Sunday   129
Twenty-eighth Sunday   131
Twenty-ninth Sunday   133
Thirtieth Sunday   136
Thirty-first Sunday   138
Thirty-second Sunday   140
Thirty-third Sunday   142
Thirty-fourth Sunday   144

Guide for the Faith
   Formation Director • 146

Preparing for the Rite
   of Election • 147

Supplement • 151

Calendar • 167

About the Authors • 176

Introduction

Dear Parent,

Welcome to *Listening to God's Word.* We hope this book will be a useful aid as you read, pray and reflect on the Sunday gospels with your child.

Purpose

This book is designed for you to use at home. It is to be used in addition to the activities your pastor or parish faith formation director may offer at your church. These parish activities are important because they help you and your child bond with the church community.

The purpose of this book is to help your child understand the Sunday gospels. It is our hope that the time you and your child spend together will be an opportunity to grow closer by learning about God, praying together and asking God's blessing on each other.

How to Use This Book

This book follows the church's calendar. It begins with Advent and ends with the feast of Christ the King, which concludes the church's year. Each week of the year has a session based on the Sunday scriptures. The title of each Sunday (such as "Third Sunday of Advent" or "Twentieth Sunday in Ordinary Time") is at the beginning of each session. The chart that begins on page 167 will help you find the right session for each week. Each session is divided into the following sections:

• The OPENING QUESTION or ACTIVITY asks you to share an experience based on the scripture theme. This can be done at any time, such as while riding in the car, at meals or before bed. It is important for both you and your child to each share your answers. It will be most enriching if both of you accept each other's feelings and thoughts without criticism or correction.

• JOURNAL questions accompany each theme. Separate adult and child journal books allow for private reflection. Sometimes you may want to share your journal, sometimes not.

• A STORY, POEM, GAME or PLAY sets the stage for understanding the scripture theme.

• A simple question invites you to TALK ABOUT THE STORY. This provides a bridge between the story and the scripture.

• SCRIPTURE is the word of God. Scripture and prayer are the most important elements of these sessions. If time is limited, omit the fiction story or game but never the scripture or prayer.

• The REFLECTION probes the meaning of the scripture, letting God's word sink into your heart.

• PRAYER is an essential element of each session because it allows time to talk *to* God rather than *about* God. This section is led by the parent. We have written a prayer you can use, but be as spontaneous and creative as you like.

• A BLESSING concludes each session. This is a time for you and your child to bless each other as you become more aware of God's loving presence in your home. Sometimes the prayer and blessing are combined.

Getting Started

You may want to read the entire book first to get an overview. This will give you an opportunity to collect materials ahead of time. If you feel that the entire contents of each week's session is too much to begin with, start small and add elements as you feel ready.

A Place for Prayer in Your Home

Many people find it helpful to have a special place for prayer and blessing (For example, if you have a family Bible, you might place it on a small table in the living room). A special tablecloth, candles, oil, water or bread could help create a prayer environment. The church uses different colors for the liturgical seasons. You might use a deep blue or purple cloth for Advent and Lent, a white cloth for Christmas and Easter, a red one for Pentecost and a green one for Ordinary Time. Some people like to listen to soft music before praying. None of this, however, is essential, so be as creative as you like.

Scheduling

Juggling schedules can be difficult. Your time may be limited. We recommend that you divide each session into two parts. For example, part one could include the Opening Question, Journal, Story and Talk About the Story sections. Part two would conclude with the Scripture, Journal, Prayer and Blessing sections. Still, these two parts might be too long for you and your child, so feel free to divide and adapt to your needs.

You may want to divide a session over several days; for example, Opening Questions could be discussed while riding in the car, at meals or at in-between times. Journaling can be done while waiting for dinner to cook or by setting aside ten minutes of each day to write. Stories and scripture can be read before tucking your child into bed. Blessings could also be part of your child's night prayer. Choose whatever fits best for your family.

Family Involvement

Though this book is designed for children nine to twelve years old, you can include other members of the family, for example, a grandparent, teenager, younger child, friend, etc. While you write in your journal, a younger child may want to participate by drawing or scribbling on an art tablet. A teenager might enjoy preparing the story and reading it out loud to the family and writing in an adult journal.

A Word of Thanks

The authors would like to thank Richelle Pearl-Koller, Sister Jeannette Lucinio and Donna Foster, who all inspired and helped in this work.

Conclusion

May God bless you as you and your child grow together in faith.

Eileen Drilling

Judy Rothfork

ADVENT

Advent means "coming." It is a four-week period before Christmas during which we Christians celebrate the coming of our Savior. Since Jesus has already come in history, the church reminds us particularly during Advent to see the presence of Jesus in our daily lives and relationships and to imitate him. Advent also prepares us for the final coming of the Lord, for which we wait and hope.

Many Catholics and other Christians mark the four weeks of waiting with an Advent wreath, a circle of evergreen branches with four candles. At dinner or at another convenient time, we light one or more candles and pray for Jesus to come.

Making an Advent Wreath

Your family may wish to make an Advent wreath for your home. You will need an evergreen wreath and four candles, three violet and one rose-colored (four white candles also work). The symbols of evergreen and a circular wreath remind us of God's everlasting love. There are four candles, each representing a week of Advent. After the wreath is blessed on the First Sunday of Advent, a prayer is prayed and one candle is lit. Each week, light an additional candle. As the light increases, we are reminded that Jesus dispels darkness.

The rose candle is lit on the Third Sunday of Advent, reminding us to rejoice, for our waiting is nearly completed. Some people replace the colored candles with white ones on Christmas. Others place a large "Christ" candle in the middle of the wreath.

If these materials are not available for you, use whatever is around the house. The idea is to help your child celebrate Christ, the light of the world.

Advent Wreath Blessing

Christ came to give us peace and happiness.
Let us pray that we may always welcome Jesus in our hearts.

Lord, hear our prayer.

That the light of Jesus may replace sadness and darkness in the world.

Lord, hear our prayer.

That this wreath may remind us of God's everlasting love.

Lord, hear our prayer.

Light one candle now and every day this week. Each week, light additional candles.

Let us pray.

God, pour your blessings on us
as we light this candle *(these candles).*
Help us to be light to each other
as Christ is the light for us all
now and forever. Amen.

First Sunday of Advent

A Time to Hope

Based on Luke 21:25–28, 34–36

Opening Question

Most of us have hopes, dreams or expectations for good things to happen. What are some of your hopes for Christmas this year? Talk about it.

Journal

See page 1, part 1 of your journal.

Story

Even when sad things happen in the world, we can have hope. Read this story about a family who placed its hope in God.

Cheering Up Aunt Liz

The week before Christmas, our house usually smells like lemon furniture polish, pine cones and fresh bread. This year, the pine smell is missing because my mother opened a thrift store on December 1, and she still hasn't had time to buy a tree.

"If we're ever going to get that tree," Mom said to me, "you'll have to help with the Christmas cleaning. And when you do the hallway, be sure to dust Dad's picture."

The next day, I stood on a kitchen chair in the hallway and, using a Q-Tip, cleaned the dust from the corners of my father's picture. He was dressed in his army uniform. I'm sure he looked right at me and smiled. He was killed in the Persian Gulf War, but that's a story I'll tell some other time.

As I dusted, I remembered a story Mom had told me and Aunt Liz a long time ago. She said that when Grandpa had stomach cancer, my father was very upset. He kept asking, "Where is God in this picture?" Dad meant that he couldn't figure out why Grandpa had to suffer so much, but I didn't know that then, so I crawled on a chair and kept staring at this picture of Dad. Mom asked, "Rag, what are you doing?" And I said, "I'm looking for God in the picture." Aunt Liz started laughing. I felt embarrassed. After all, I was only four years old at the time.

As I dusted, I was so lost in my thoughts that I nearly fell off the chair when the phone rang. I expected it to be my friend Erin calling about our geography project, but it was Aunt Liz.

"Rag, get your mom on the other phone. There is something I want both of you to hear."

"Mom," I yelled, but she was already on the line.

"Oh, Betty, and you too, Rag, Len has to go to Bosnia to be a peacekeeper." I watch the news, so I knew what that meant. "War again," I sighed to myself. But at least keeping peace seemed better than fighting. Then Mom and Aunt Liz both began to cry.

"I'm so sorry," my mother said, "and right before Christmas, too."

"Aunt Liz," I interrupted, "why don't you come to our house for Christmas?"

"Yes, Liz, do. And come as soon as you can. Stay with us awhile. It gets lonesome here during the holidays."

Two days after the phone call, I was sitting on my bed doing homework. I had just about given up trying to divide 2,478 by 64 when I heard a loud honk. I looked out the window and saw my Aunt Liz standing by the open trunk of her red car. She was holding a pair of high-heeled, black leather boots in one hand and a hammer and saw in the other. I grabbed my jacket and raced out to help her.

Mom was working late at the thrift shop, so Aunt Liz and I carried everything to the guest room. I eyed her two big suitcases, and I knew she was planning to stay a few weeks.

When she finished unpacking, she said, "Come on, Rag, let's surprise your mom and get a tree!" We bought a huge one. It was so tall that it reached the highest point of our living room ceiling. That's Aunt Liz. Whatever she does is different and better than what I expect.

The next morning, I found out why she had brought her hammer and saw. The two of us found some old boards, cardboard boxes and paint in the basement. Aunt Liz cut out figures of Jesus, Mary and Joseph, and I painted them. We made two shepherds, a sheep, an ox and a donkey; then we took everything outside. When we finished working, our manger scene covered most of the front lawn. We outlined everything with green, yellow, blue and red lights.

We were a family, Mom, Aunt Liz and I. And I knew this would be my best Christmas ever. That evening, I squeezed all the packages under the tree, hoping one would be a pair of jeans for me. I could see Aunt Liz sitting by the window staring at the darkness. Mom said to me, "I feel bad for Liz. I know she misses your Uncle Len a lot."

After Dad died, I learned that I could make Mom laugh if I tried hard enough. I was sure that I could make Aunt Liz feel better, too. I brought out my cartoon collection. We had a contest to see who could find the funniest one. Mom was the judge.

On Christmas Eve, my favorite day of the whole year, I especially wanted Aunt Liz to be in good spirits. I started telling her knock-knock jokes. Mom called me into the kitchen.

"Rag, don't work so hard to keep Liz laughing. It's okay for her to be sad once in a while. Come and help me decorate the sugar cookies."

A little later, my aunt came into the kitchen to help frost cookies. She made each cookie look like someone we knew.

"This is what Christmas should feel like," I thought as we laughed and nibbled and sang along with our favorite carols on the radio. Then the music stopped. "Breaking news from Bosnia," said the voice. "An American soldier has been wounded in a land-mine explosion. The extent of his injuries is still unknown."

Aunt Liz gave a little scream and snapped off the radio. I started to follow her out of the kitchen, but Mom shook her head, no.

"Let her go, Rag," she said, "she needs some time." I could see my aunt from the kitchen door. She was sitting on the steps in the dark hallway, her arms around her knees.

When we finished decorating the cookies, Mom said, "You can sit with her now, Rag."

I sat on the steps next to Aunt Liz. I wanted to cheer her up, but I remembered what Mom had told me about letting her be sad sometimes. But after awhile I couldn't stand seeing her so pale and quiet. I pointed to the big picture of Dad. "Look, Aunt Liz," I said. "Where do you think God is in this picture?" I had hoped she would remember Mom's story and laugh. Instead, she took my hand and began to sob. I was stunned. Christmas was turning out just terrible. I looked up. My aunt's eyes were wet, but they looked soft and beautiful.

"Rag, you're right," she smiled. "God is in the picture. God is taking care of Len better than I could. Let's just sit here and think about God taking care of your Uncle Len."

We sat together quietly until I fell asleep. The ringing of the phone jarred me awake. I jumped up, but Aunt Liz grabbed the phone first.

"Hello," I heard her say. "Len, you're okay! I knew it. Rag helped me remember that God is with you and taking care of you. I love you so much."

I looked up at Dad's photograph and smiled back at him. Christmas would be just fine with God in the picture.

First Sunday of Advent

Talk About the Story

If you were Rag, what would you have said to Aunt Liz to give her hope when she was sad? Has someone ever encouraged you when you were unhappy? What did that person say or do?

Scripture

The writers of the Bible often used images of nature's power. They also tell us that God has even more power. Read Luke 21:25 – 28, 34 – 36 and see how this gospel writer encouraged people to hope in God.

A reading from the holy gospel according to Luke

Jesus said to his disciples: "Strange things will happen to the sun, moon, and stars. The nations on earth will be afraid of the roaring sea and tides, and they won't know what to do. People will be so frightened that they will faint because of what is happening to the world. Every power in the sky will be shaken.

"Then the Son of Man will be seen, coming in a cloud with great power and glory. When all of this starts happening, stand up straight and be brave. You will soon be set free.

"Don't spend all of your time thinking about eating or drinking or worrying about life. If you do, the final day will suddenly catch you like a trap. That day will surprise everyone on earth.

"Watch out and keep praying that you can escape all that is going to happen and that the Son of Man will be pleased with you."

The gospel of the Lord.

Reflection

If you were to experience any of these powers of nature, how would you feel? What would you say to God? What would God say to you?

Journal

See page 1, part 2 of your journal.

Prayer

Place your journal books on the prayer table. Light a candle (or the first candle of an Advent wreath, if you have one) while saying:

Jesus, you are the light of the world.
You bring hope to all people.
Help each of us to be a light
by encouraging others during Advent.

Blessing

Pass the lighted candle from person to person, saying:

(Name), have hope, the Light of Christ is always with you.

Second Sunday of Advent

A Time to Prepare

Based on Luke 3:1 – 6

Opening Question

What kinds of things has our family done to prepare for someone's arrival (for example, a new baby, special guest, relative or friend)?

Story

Here is a story about some children preparing for a very special person (pronunciation note: *madre* = MAHdray, which is Spanish for mother).

The Madre Is Coming

"Today I will not work in the cornfield," Alberto told Tomás as they watched a wild parrot swoop down from a tree for its share of the corn. "We need to help decorate the poles for the fiesta. And I want to practice my marimba solo one more time."

This was a very important day at the orphanage where Alberto and his brother, Tomás, lived. A madre was coming. Though Señora Maria and her oldest daughter, Julia, helped cook the meals and care for the children, today, for the first time, a madre (mother) would come to live with them.

As they hurried home from school, Alberto remembered the day four years ago when his Uncle José had brought him and Tomás across the lake to live at the orphanage on the mountainside. He still shuddered when he thought of the illness that had killed their father and mother. "I don't understand such sickness," he said aloud. Brushing a tear away with his shirt sleeve, he put his arm around his brother. "Today we will have a new mother," Alberto assured him. But inside he wondered, what will she be like? Will she be kind?

Tomás kicked bits of mud to the side as they walked along. "I don't want the madre to get her shoes dirty," he explained. Alberto smiled. He knew the older children had spent hours yesterday getting the mile-long path from the road to the *casa*, the house, ready for the madre. But he also knew how much Tomás wanted to help. So he didn't say anything. Hadn't Alberto himself offered to carry the madre's suitcase on his back up the mountainside? But Señora Maria said, "No, you are still too small."

By two o'clock, Alberto and Tomás were back at the *casa* cutting strips of cloth to make brightly colored banners. Julia showed Tomás how to attach the strips to a pole decorated with flowers. When the madre arrived, he would stand with the other children, each carrying a pole along the entryway. "Mm-mmm," Tomás murmured. He closed his eyes and licked his lips as he smelled the breads and cakes baking. What a fiesta they had planned!

Alberto had just begun practicing his marimba solo when the earth shook. The orphanage, with its walls of volcanic rock and cement floor, was not damaged by such a small earthquake. But Alberto's throat tightened and his hands trembled when he thought of his uncle's thatched hut. Had the tremor toppled Uncle José's home?

Then Alberto's mind raced to the newly cleaned path. Mud from the mountainside, stirred by the movement of the earth, would once more cover the path. Alberto knew. He had seen it happen before.

"The path! The path!" he cried. "It's covered with mud. We must clean it again for the madre."

Grabbing sticks and shovels, anything they could find, the children ran to the path.

It was five o'clock when the first of the shovelers straggled back, sweat running from their tired but jubilant faces.

"The path is ready and the madre is here!" they shouted.

Two men came first, each one carrying a suitcase on his back. Next came the madre, escorted by the two oldest girls. Alberto studied the madre's face intently. A light radiated from her soft brown eyes. Smile-wrinkles moved out from the sides of her mouth when she talked. "She's beautiful," he whispered to Tomás, and he squeezed his brother's shoulder.

The entryway seemed alive as the children, dressed in their best clothes, held the green, blue, orange and red poles. Alberto grabbed his marimba sticks, and the mountainside rang with the song of welcome. Never had he played so well.

Only when the song was finished did he stop to catch his breath and look up. The madre was smiling at him.

"My children, *gracias*. You have worked hard to prepare the path and make my homecoming special. I am happy to be with you."

Alberto, Tomás and all of the children encircled the madre and entered the *casa*. The fiesta had begun.

Talk About the Story

What would it be like to be one of the children in this story? How would you prepare for the madre's coming?

Journal

See page 2, part 1 of your journal.

Scripture

In your journal, you wrote about your own history. When you read the first two verses of today's gospel (Luke 3:1–2), you will hear about John the Baptist's place in history. John helped the people prepare for Jesus' coming. In the remaining verses (3–6), you will see how he did that.

A reading from the holy gospel according to Luke

For fifteen years Emperor Tiberius had ruled that part of the world, and Annas and Caiaphas were the Jewish high priests. At that time God spoke to Zechariah's son John, who was living in the desert.

So John went along the Jordan Valley, telling the people, "Turn back to God and be baptized! Then your sins will be forgiven." Isaiah the prophet wrote about John when he said,

"In the desert someone is shouting,
'Get the road ready for the Lord!
Make a straight path for him!
Fill up every valley and level every mountain and hill.
Straighten the crooked paths and smooth out the rough roads.
Then everyone will see the saving power of God.'"

The gospel of the Lord.

Reflection

Imagine yourself meeting John the Baptist. What would he be like? What might he say to you? (Parent, you may need to coach a little.)

Optional Activity

Choose one or more of the following activities as a way to prepare for Jesus' coming. Explain that when we do things together, we "make ready the way of the Lord."

1. With your child, begin making some Christmas plans. Write a list of preparation tasks. Then ask your child to volunteer for some of them. Be encouraging, and thank your child for helping with these preparations.

2. Decide together who you would like to have as a guest(s). Write a list of preparation tasks. Divide the responsibilities so that the "rough ways are made smooth."

3. With your child, buy or make a Christmas gift to share with someone. You may want to check if your church or community is collecting toys, food or other gifts for those in need.

Journal

See page 2, part 2 of your journal.

Prayer

Reverently place a Bible on the prayer table. Then put your journals on top of the Bible while saying:

Jesus, thank you for taking a place in history.
Thank you for being in our history, too.
Help us to prepare our hearts to celebrate your birth at Christmas.

Blessing

Light a candle (or two purple candles on the Advent wreath). Then take the candle and pass it from person to person, saying:

(Name), you are the light of Christ. Amen.

Third Sunday of Advent

A Time to Give

Based on Luke 3:10 – 14

Opening Question

If you could receive any gift in the whole world, what would you want? If you could give any gift in the whole world, what would you give?

Activity

At times we may give more than what is expected (for example, when we surprise each other with small acts of love). For a special Christmas gift this year, you might give a little bit of yourself, which is the best gift of all. In your journal (child's) you will find a sample gift certificate. You might want to make certificates for family and friends.

Journal

See page 3, part 1 of your journal.

Scripture

God is constantly giving gifts. The people in today's gospel want to give God a gift in return. John the Baptist gives them some ideas. Read Luke 3:10 – 14.

> **A reading from the holy gospel according to Luke**
>
> The crowds asked John the Baptist, "What should we do?"
> John told them, "If you have two coats, give one to someone who doesn't have any. If you have food, share it with someone else."
> When tax collectors came to be baptized, they asked John, "Teacher, what should we do?" John told them, "Don't make people pay more than they owe."
> Some soldiers asked him, "And what about us? What do we have to do?"
> John told them, "Don't force people to pay money to make you leave them alone. Be satisfied with your pay."
>
> **The gospel of the Lord.**

Reflection

How might John the Baptist answer if you asked him, "What should I do?"

Journal

See page 3, part 2 of your journal.

Prayer

God, generous gift-giver,
we thank you for all your gifts,
even those we never asked for.
You have given us the gift of nature,
the gifts of each other,
gifts of school and work.

Parents, mention gifts for which you are grateful. Then ask your child, "Is there a gift you would like to add to our prayer?" Pause for a response, then continue with the blessing.

Blessing

Light a candle (or if you have an Advent wreath, light three candles — two purple and one rose). Pass the (rose) candle from person to person, saying:

(Name), rejoice, for God loves you.

Fourth Sunday of Advent

A Time to Trust

Based on Luke 1:39–45

Opening Activity

Tell your child that you are going to play a game in which you take turns blindfolding each other and leading each other through an obstacle course. Blindfold your child and then rearrange a few pieces of the furniture in two of the rooms of your home. Next, gently turn your child around three times and carefully lead him or her around the furniture, assuring the child that he or she will not bump into anything.

When you are finished, have your child do the same with you. Then ask each other: What was it like to be blindfolded? Were you able to trust? Why or why not?

Journal

See page 4, part 1 of your journal.

Scripture

In today's scripture, you will read about two women who trusted in God. Read Luke 1:39–45.

A reading from the holy gospel according to Luke

Mary hurried to a town in the hill country of Judea. She went into Zechariah's home, where she greeted Elizabeth. When Elizabeth heard Mary's greeting, her baby moved within her.

The Holy Spirit came upon Elizabeth. Then in a loud voice she said to Mary: "God has blessed you more than any other woman! He has also blessed the child you will have. Why should the mother of my Lord come to me? As soon as I heard your greeting, my baby became happy and moved within me. The Lord has blessed you because you believed that he will keep his promise."

The gospel of the Lord.

Reflection

If I were Mary, I would _____ .
If I were Elizabeth, I would _____ .

Journal

See page 4, part 2 of your journal.

Optional Activities for Christmas

See the supplement in the back of this book for a dramatization of the Christmas story and other family activities.

Prayer

Light all four candles on your Advent wreath, and then pray:

God, we thank you for the greatest gift of all, Jesus.
Help us to be like Mary, who had so much faith and trust in you.
Increase our faith as we bless each other.

Blessing

Bless each other on the forehead, saying:

(Name), God loves you. May your faith in God grow stronger every day.

Christmas Season

On the church's calendar, Christmas is more than just one day. It is a whole season during which we celebrate all the ways that Jesus lived as a human being and continues to live among his people.

Throughout the centuries, Christians have found ways to extend the celebration of Christmas. Special foods, special gifts, special songs and other customs grew up around this time. This is the origin of the "Twelve Days of Christmas." Some Christians have their festive meals and exchange gifts on the feast of the Epiphany. If you can, this would be a good time to find some books in the library about how Christmas is celebrated in different places. Perhaps some of the older members of your family or your parish could tell some stories of Christmas traditions.

You and your child might choose together how to celebrate all of Christmas. These celebrations don't have to be big or elaborate: perhaps making a special food, praying a special prayer together, keeping the Christmas tree up longer or lighting a Christmas candle at supper each night. Then remember to do it again next year. That's how traditions get started.

CHRISTMAS

The Christmas Story

Luke 2:1 – 14

A reading from the holy gospel according to Luke

Emperor Augustus gave orders for the names of all the people to be listed in record books. These first records were made when Quirinius was governor of Syria.

Everyone had to go to their own hometown to be listed. So Joseph had to leave Nazareth in Galilee and go to Bethlehem in Judea. Long ago Bethlehem had been King David's hometown, and Joseph went there because he was from David's family.

Mary was engaged to Joseph and traveled with him to Bethlehem. She was soon going to have a baby, and while they were there, she gave birth to her first-born son. She dressed him in baby clothes and laid him in a manger, because there was no room for them in the inn.

That night in the fields near Bethlehem some shepherds were guarding their sheep. All at once an angel came down to them from the Lord, and the brightness of the Lord's glory flashed around them. The shepherds were frightened. But the angel said, "Don't be afraid! I have good news for you, which will make everyone happy. This very day in King David's hometown a Savior was born for you. He is Christ the Lord. You will know who he is because you will find him dressed in baby clothes and lying in a manger."

Suddenly many other angels came down from heaven and joined in praising God. They said: "Praise God in heaven! Peace on earth to everyone who pleases God."

The gospel of the Lord.

Journal

See page 5, parts 1 and 2 of your journal.

Optional Activities

There are other Christmas activities that you and your child may enjoy in the supplement of this book.

Holy Family

Based on Matthew 2:13–15, 19–23

Opening Question

There are many kinds of families: two-parent families, single-parent families, families with more than two parents, parents and children living with aunts, uncles or grandparents. Who is included in your family? What are some things you like about your family?

Journal

See page 6, part 1 of your journal.

Story

Here is a story about a girl who discovered that her family was willing to help and support her.

The Gift

Judy yawned and folded back the brown wool blanket. Then she remembered, "I'm the new class president." She jumped out of bed, splashed water on her face and pulled on her jeans and sweater.

After brushing her long, curly hair, Judy reached into her top dresser drawer and took out a red and yellow coin purse. The eyes of the circus clown on the front of the purse stared at her seriously.

"I know," Judy said to herself as she stuffed the empty purse into her sweater pocket. "Being class president is a serious responsibility. And today I will begin by collecting money for Mrs. Olson's Christmas present."

After breakfast, Chris and Pat were waiting for her on the gray stone bench on the street corner, as usual.

"I wonder what we should get Mrs. Olson for Christmas," Judy said as the three boarded the bus for school. "It has to be something special. She's the best teacher we've ever had."

"I know," Pat replied. "Let's ask Ms. Stevens. She and Mrs. Olson are always talking together."

When the bus arrived at school, the three girls went straight to Ms. Stevens' sixth-grade classroom. Ms. Stevens put her work down and listened to Judy's question.

"Why, she just told me yesterday that she needs a new alarm clock," Ms. Stevens said, "and I know she likes blue."

Judy, Chris and Pat giggled and whispered about the secret gift as they walked to their own classroom.

"Here's fifty cents," Chris said, as she handed Judy two quarters.

"And here's some more," Pat joined in, after she unearthed three dimes and two pennies from her faded orange pencil case. Judy dropped the money into her coin purse and carefully placed it back into her sweater pocket. By the end of the day, the face of the clown on the purse was bulging like the cheeks of a fat squirrel.

"We've collected 14 dollars and 32 cents," Judy announced to the class after the three girls counted the money. "I'll buy the blue alarm clock on Saturday."

The money had to be kept in a safe place until the weekend. Judy knew exactly where she would hide it.

"Mm-mmm, chocolate chip cookies," Judy murmured as she walked into the kitchen after school. She helped herself to three of them. Then she pulled a chair over to the refrigerator, peered on top and carefully nestled the purse among all the other important papers the family kept there. "It will be safe there until Saturday morning," she said to herself as she climbed down. Then Judy called Greene's Hardware Store to ask about the gift.

"We have a blue alarm clock for 11 dollars," the clerk told her.

"Perfect," Judy thought. She would buy it while her mother was getting her hair styled at Millie's Beauty Salon.

On Friday evening, Judy was so excited about buying the gift that she was still awake at midnight. When she did finally fall asleep, she dreamed about a blue alarm clock that danced and sang, and then rang so loudly that it woke her up. The luminous hands of her own clock pierced the darkness of her room.

"Only five o'clock," Judy thought. "I can't wait any longer." She tiptoed to the kitchen. The smell of last night's popcorn made her thirsty. The water gurgled as she turned on the faucet. The refrigerator was humming. Everything in the kitchen seemed to sing, "We're so happy to be carrying the secret of the gift." Judy's heart sang, too, as she climbed up on a chair to retrieve the money. She rummaged among the papers on the top of the refrigerator. Her heart started to race.

"I put it right here," she thought. She searched again, but the red and yellow purse was no longer nestled among the family treasures. It had disappeared.

Judy felt sick. What would she tell Chris and Pat? What about all the classmates who had entrusted their money to her? Now there would be no blue alarm clock for Mrs. Olson. She had let everyone down. Then she had an idea.

Judy ran back to her bedroom and pulled out a yellow elephant bank from her bottom dresser drawer. She would have to spend the money she had saved to buy Christmas presents for her parents. She pried open the bank and frantically counted the money.

"Ten dollars, 11, 12, 13, 14," she counted. "Thank you, Jesus," she sighed. There was enough money to buy the clock and the card.

"Judy, you're so quiet this morning," her mother said later as the two drove to the mall.

"I'm all right." Judy tried to smile. She couldn't tell her mother that she had failed in her first job as the new class president. She would tell no one.

And so she bought the clock. But the secret wasn't fun anymore. She felt sad and alone. It was a very long weekend.

Then Monday after school, Judy was surprised to see her father's van parked in the driveway. "Why is Dad home so early?" she wondered. "He's never home at this time." But there he was in the living room, sitting in the worn leather armchair, sipping coffee and talking quietly with her mother.

"Judy, come here," her father said softly. "Do you know anything about this?" He was holding up the bulging coin purse.

"You found it!" Judy exclaimed. "I didn't know what to do. I spent all my own money for Mrs. Olson's present." She took the purse and hugged it to herself. "Now I can buy you and Mom Christmas presents." Her eyes were wet with tears as she finally told her parents the story of the lost purse.

Judy's mother looked at her with a puzzled expression on her face. "But Judy, why didn't you tell us that you lost the money?"

"I couldn't. It was my job to keep it safe, and I failed. How could I tell anyone that?"

"Judy, you don't have to be alone. You can always come to us for help," her mother assured her.

Her father hugged her and said, "We can help you with money or anything you need. We are your family."

"I'm not alone," Judy thought as she skipped to her room. She smiled as she stuffed the money into the yellow elephant bank. "What should I get Mom and Dad for Christmas?" she wondered. "It has to be something special. They are my family."

Talk About the Story

If you were Judy or her parents, how would you have felt?

Scripture

Today's gospel is about two parents who were concerned for their child's safety. Read Matthew 2:13–15, 19–23.

> A reading from the holy gospel according to Matthew
>
> An angel from the Lord appeared to Joseph in a dream. The angel said, "Get up! Hurry and take the child and his mother to Egypt! Stay there until I tell you to return, because Herod is looking for the child and wants to kill him."
>
> That night Joseph got up and took his wife and the child to Egypt, where they stayed until Herod died. So the Lord's promise came true, just as the prophet had said, "I called my son out of Egypt."
>
> After King Herod died, an angel from the Lord appeared in a dream to Joseph while he was still in Egypt. The angel said, "Get up and take the child and his mother back to Israel. The people who wanted to kill him are now dead."
>
> Joseph got up and left with them for Israel. But when he heard that Herod's son Archelaus was now ruler of Judea, he was afraid to go there. Then in a dream he was told to go to Galilee, and they went to live there in the town of Nazareth.
>
> So the Lord's promise came true, just as the prophet had said, "He will be called a Nazarene."
>
> The gospel of the Lord.

Reflection

Imagine you are Mary, Joseph or Herod. Tell about your experience.

Journal

See page 6, part 2 of your journal.

Prayer

Let us pray.
God, you are a nurturing parent.
Thank you for our family.
Each one of us is precious.
Help us to love and care for each other.

Blessing

Place your hands on your child's head, and pray the prayer you wrote in your journal. (If others are present, invite them to surround the child and share the prayers they prepared also.) Do this with each member of the family.

Mary, Mother of God

Based on Luke 2:16–21

Opening Question

Christmas is a time to let others know how special they are. We often give cards and gifts to let people know that they are a blessing in our lives. What are some ways people show you that you are a blessing to them? How do they let you know that they care about you?

Journal

See page 7, part 1 of your journal.

Scripture

On January 1, the church celebrates the feast of Mary, Mother of God. Read Luke 2:16–21 to see why Mary is a blessing to us.

> A reading from the holy gospel according to Luke
>
> The shepherds hurried off and found Mary and Joseph, and they saw the baby lying in the manger.
>   When the shepherds saw Jesus, they told his parents what the angel had said about him. Everyone listened and was surprised. But Mary kept thinking about all this and wondering what it meant.
>   As the shepherds returned to their sheep, they were praising God and saying wonderful things about him. Everything they had seen and heard was just as the angel had said.
>   Eight days later Jesus' parents did for him what the Law of Moses commands. And they named him Jesus, just as the angel had told Mary when he promised she would have a baby.
>
> The gospel of the Lord.

Reflection

Imagine that you are with the Holy Family in the stable. What would you be saying in your heart?

Journal

See page 7, part 2 of your journal.

Activity

Choose one or both of the following activities.

A. Write thank-you notes to family and friends who were blessings to you this Christmas.

B. If your child does not know the "Hail Mary," help him or her memorize this common prayer using the following:

1) The angel of the Lord came to Mary and said:
> Hail Mary, full of grace,
> the Lord is with you!

2) Mary went to visit her cousin Elizabeth, who greeted her saying:
> "Blessed are you among women,
> and blessed is the fruit of your womb."

Then ask your child, "Who is the fruit of Mary's womb?"
(Pause for, or prompt, the word "Jesus.")

3) The church adds a little more to the prayer. It goes like this:
> Holy Mary, mother of God,
> pray for us sinners,
> now and at the hour of our death. Amen.

This is a prayer we can say to Mary, the Mother of God. It reminds us of how Mary is a blessing to us.

Prayer

If you have a statue or picture of Mary, place it on the prayer table. Gather around the table, and pray:

God, you always bless us
with wonderful gifts.
Thank you for the blessing of Mary,
the mother of Jesus.

We honor Mary today by praying together:

Hail Mary, full of grace,
the Lord is with you!
Blessed are you among women,
and blessed is the fruit of your womb, Jesus.
Holy Mary, mother of God,
pray for us sinners,
now and at the hour of our death. Amen.

Blessing

Give each other a hug while saying:

(Name), you are God's blessing to me.

EPIPHANY

Jesus Is for Everyone

Based on Matthew 2:1–12

Opening Question

Tell about a time when you felt left out. For example, it may have been a time when others kept secrets from you or didn't want to share with you.

Journal

See page 8, part 1 of your journal.

Scripture

A long time ago, when the Gospel of Matthew was written, some people didn't want to share Jesus. So Matthew included in his gospel a story to help them understand that Jesus came to everyone, not just to one nation. Here is a play that tells this story. It is adapted from Matthew 2:1–12. If you have a smaller family, some of you may need to take more than one part. There are seven characters: Herod, King 1, King 2, King 3, Joseph, Priest, Narrator.

The Three Kings from the East

Scene 1

Narrator   King Herod ruled the land when Jesus was born. Herod was a cruel king. One day, three other kings visited him in the palace. These kings studied stars and had noticed a beautiful, bright new star in the sky.

The kings enter the palace and stand before Herod.

King 1   Where is the newborn king of the Jews?

King 2   We have seen his star.

King 3   We have come to pay him homage.

Herod   *(Surprised and hiding his jealousy)* Oh, I haven't noticed any star. But please stay and eat. You must be very tired and hungry. I'll ask the chief priests and scribes what they know about it.

King 1   Thank you for your kindness.

King 2   We can stay for a little while.

King 3   We are eager to find the new king.

The three kings exit.

Herod   *(Angrily talking to a servant)* Call in the chief priests and scribes. What do they know about a star and a newborn king? Hurry up. *(Servant exits. King talks to himself.)* What could this mean? I must not let the people know how upset I am. I'll pretend to be interested in this newborn king. But once I find him, I'll have him killed.

Priest	Your Majesty *(bows before Herod)*, we looked in the scriptures and found that the prophet Isaiah said that a ruler of the people would be born in Bethlehem.
Herod	*(Angrily)* Aren't they finished eating yet? Go and tell them that we have the answer to their question. That will make them hurry. *(Chief priest exits. Herod talks and grumbles to himself.)* I don't want any king to get in my way. I am the ruler of this nation. I'll kill him before people hear about this newborn king.

The three kings enter.

King 1	What a generous meal we had!
King 2	You are so kind!
King 3	What news did you hear about the newborn king?
Herod	The chief priests and scribes found that the prophet Isaiah mentioned something about a ruler being born at this time in history. He should be found in Bethlehem. Go and get detailed information about the child. When you have discovered something, report your findings to me so that I may go and offer him homage too.
King 1	We will be very happy to tell you what we have seen.
King 2	Again, we thank you for your kindness.
King 3	Come, let us not waste any time.

The three kings exit.

Scene 2

Narrator	Scene two. The three kings follow Herod's directions and go to Bethlehem, where they follow the star to a small shack.
King 3	*(Knocks on the door)* Let us find the new king here.
Joseph	*(Joseph opens the door and is amazed at the splendor of the kings.)* Why, please come in.
King 1	We have come to pay homage to the newborn king.
King 2	We have see his star in the sky. *(Joseph carries Jesus over to the kings. All three kings kneel down in worship.)*
King 3	Little King, we bring gifts of gold, frankincense and myrrh, for you are to be the salvation of all nations.
Narrator	That night, the kings received a message in a dream not to return to Herod, so they went back to their own country by another route. The good news of Jesus was spread to all nations.

Reflection

Imagine that you were one of the kings. Tell about your long journey, your visit with Herod and your meeting with Jesus and his family.

Journal

See page 8, part 2 of your journal.

Prayer

If you have the three kings, let your child place them in the nativity scene. You and your child may want to share the prayers written on page 10 of your journals.

Blessing

Give a hug and a blessing to each other while saying:

(Name), **you have shown the goodness of Jesus. Thank you. May God continue to bless you.**

BAPTISM OF THE LORD

Based on Luke 3:15–16, 21–22

Opening Question

Name the different groups, teams or organizations to which you belong (for example, your grade in school, sports teams, scouts, business, political groups, etc.). What is the purpose of each group?

Journal

See page 9, part 1 of your journal.

Story

Today's story takes place in Rome during the first century after Jesus' birth. It is about a boy and his family who wanted to belong to the group that followed Jesus' way. Read the story to see how they became Christians.

Marcus Is Baptized

"I am the luckiest boy in all of Rome," Marcus thought, for tonight Peter himself would baptize him. He leaned over the marble railing on the staircase and watched a servant carry a large silver tray of grapes to a long table on the other side of the pool. The pool brought a tinge of fear and sadness to his excitement. Thoughts of his little brother, Lucas, struggling for air flashed through his mind. Athough Lucas had not drowned that day a year ago, Marcus remembered with shame that he had panicked and had run away.

He brushed aside the memories of Lucas. But it was harder to stop the uneasy feeling that made his breathing shallow when he saw the cold, dark water. He was determined, though, that tonight the water would be his friend.

"Mm-mmm," he said to himself as he smelled the ducks roasting on the spit. Servants were bustling back and forth, lighting lamps and setting out the wine. A table with trays of fruit and honeycakes had been set up on the other side of the pool.

The aroma was too great to resist. Marcus raced down the stairs, ran around the pool and grabbed a honeycake.

"Marcus, those are for your party," his mother chided, but he was already up the stairs and out of sight.

Marcus inspected the white toga hanging in his room as he munched on the honeycake. Tonight he would wear it for the first time after he was baptized. He heard a commotion downstairs and recognized Peter's voice.

Marcus ran through the parlor, down the stairway and out to the atrium where Peter was standing. Marcus was surprised to see his friend Claudius in the small group that had come with Peter. It was dangerous to be openly Christian in Rome.

Peter's dark, friendly eyes peered out from a face almost hidden by a bushy beard.

"Hello, Marcus. Are you ready to become one of us?"

"Yes, I know I am ready," he said eagerly.

"Well, then, let's begin," Peter exclaimed. He gathered the group together and prayed, "Lord, with praise and thanksgiving we celebrate the work you have begun in this family. With your love and spirit, they are ready to join our Christian community. We are grateful that you have invited this family to follow you. Holy Lord God, you have graced us with your goodness again and again. Bless all these witnesses of your Son, Jesus. Help each of us to be strong in our conviction that you are the one and true God. Your name is holy."

Then Peter motioned all but the family to move to the other side of the pool. First Marcus' father was baptized, then his mother. Then Peter took Marcus by the hand and led him down the steps. Before his feet even touched the water, Marcus's legs refused to move any further. He looked at his brother Lucas waiting next to the pool for his turn. The memories raced through his mind.

"Don't be afraid," Peter urged gently, but Marcus pulled free of Peter's hand and fled into the hall and up the staircase.

Later, Peter found him crouched by his bed crying.

"I'm so ashamed," he sobbed. "I am a coward, afraid of a little water."

Peter's eyes were gentle. "I understand. You are not a coward. It takes a brave person to become a Christian in Rome. But it is because of Lucas that you are afraid of the water."

Marcus dried a tear with his sleeve. "But you are so brave, Peter."

Peter looked kindly at the boy. "I was once afraid of the water, too. I began to sink, and I screamed with terror. Jesus helped me. Jesus will help you, too." Peter stood up and walked toward the door. "There are still some honeycakes left. Come and join the others."

Marcus hesitated, remembering that his friend Claudius had seen him run away. "I am ashamed to face them," he said.

Peter reached for his belt and showed Marcus a wooden cross, which was fastened to a loop of leather. "Marcus, I made this cross from a tree in the Garden of Olives. That's where Jesus prayed the night before he died. Jesus was afraid too. He told me so himself. I carry this cross to remind myself that it won't always be easy to follow Jesus. I want you to wear it after you are baptized."

"Can I take it into the water with me?" Marcus asked.

"Yes," Peter answered.

"Then I want to be baptized tonight."

As Peter and Marcus walked down the steps into the water for the second time that night, Marcus clutched the wooden cross in his hand. "Help me to be brave, Jesus," he kept repeating to himself. When his feet touched the water, his legs felt shaky. He closed his eyes and prayed. The water closed over his head, and he felt as if he were buried in a tomb.

"Here he comes," his mother cried excitedly as he came out of the pool, shaking water from his hair and eyes. His father brought the fresh white toga and slipped it over Marcus's shoulders. Peter took the cross from Marcus's hand and put the leather loop around his neck. The atrium rang with song and prayer. It was then that Marcus knew Jesus would always give him the strength he needed to be a Christian.

Talk About the Story

If you were Marcus, what would you have remembered most about that night? If you were one of the Christians, what would you have said to Marcus?

Scripture

This scripture tells about the day Jesus was baptized. Imagine that you are in the story.

A reading from the holy gospel according to Luke

Everyone became excited and wondered, "Could John be the Messiah?"

John said, "I am just baptizing with water. But someone more powerful is going to come, and I am not good enough even to untie his sandals. He will baptize you with the Holy Spirit and with fire."

After everyone else had been baptized, Jesus himself was baptized. Then as he prayed, the sky opened up, and the Holy Spirit came down upon him in the form of a dove. A voice from heaven said, "You are my own dear Son, and I am pleased with you."

The gospel of the Lord.

Reflection

If I had been by the River Jordan that day, I would have _____ .

Journal

See page 9, part 2 of your journal.

Prayer

Place a small bowl of water on the prayer table. Then begin with this prayer:

Jesus, thank you for inviting us
to be your followers.
Please give us your spirit
so that we may always live
with love and courage. Amen.

Blessing

Dip your hand into the water and bless each other, saying:

May you be blessed.
In the name of the Father, and of the Son, and of the Holy Spirit. Amen.

LENT

Lent is a time of preparation. During Lent, those who are going to be baptized at Easter spend time getting ready for that big change in their lives. They pray. They listen to scripture. They fast. They give money to the poor. They repent of their sins.

During Lent, the rest of the church is getting ready to receive those who are going to be baptized as brothers and sisters in Christ and is getting ready to renew their own baptismal promises. So they, also, pray, listen to scripture, fast, give money to the poor and repent of their sins.

Discuss with your child ways that your family can keep Lent together. Perhaps your parish takes part in a program of fasting and collecting money for the poor, such as Catholic Relief Services' *Rice Bowl* program.

Many Catholics practice the custom of giving up something for Lent. Others do something positive. When both are combined, such as by giving up an hour of television to spend it helping someone, it is especially good.

The time we spend preparing during Lent benefits us not only at Easter but all year long.

First Sunday of Lent

God Is Our Strength

Based on Luke 4:1 – 13

Opening Activity

Ask each member of the family to tell how it feels when he or she says "no" to a friend.

Journal

See page 10, part 1 of your journal.

Story

Today's story is about a boy who was tempted to do something wrong in order to be a good buddy to his brother. He had a big decision to make.

The Temptation

"Quit snooping around and get out of here," Pete growled at his younger brother. He slammed the door of his bedroom and locked it.

Josh walked with drooping shoulders down the narrow hallway toward his room. He stopped to glare at a picture of Pete, whose face looked radiant in the sunlight as he clutched a baseball trophy. "Some hero," Josh muttered through his teeth. Brushing his baseball cards to one side of the bed, he sat cross-legged, head in his hands. He was sure he had smelled liquor on Pete's breath again.

What was happening? These hours after school used to be the best part of the day. Pete had seldom been crabby then. Both their parents worked until six o'clock at the hardware store. While they waited for them to come home, Josh and Pete would wrestle on the living room floor or play soccer. Josh even liked hanging around the kitchen, helping Pete peel potatoes or shred cabbage for supper. One night his mother's list of chores had read: "Peel pot. Put wine vin. on lettuce." "Hey, we're having marijuana and wine for supper," Pete had joked. And the two rolled on the floor with laughter.

Now Pete was drinking, and there was nothing funny about it at all. It was terrifying. Josh hugged his knees to his chest. He rocked back and forth, trying to still his quivering body. These last four months had been so hard. Nothing was the way it used to be. Pete was crabby most of the time. If he wasn't arguing with his parents, he was locked in his room. Josh began to sob, allowing the fear and loneliness to sweep over him.

A shadow in the doorway startled him. "Hi Buddy." Pete was standing there. "I'm sorry I've been a little edgy lately."

"Sure, since you started drinking," Josh thought bitterly. "Why can't I say it out loud?" he wondered.

Soon they were on the floor wrestling. It seemed like old times, but the past months had taught Josh to be wary. He never knew what Pete's mood would be. Then something fell out of his brother's pocket: a skinny twisted cigarette.

"That's a joint!" Josh exclaimed in surprise. "Now, now, is the time to say it," a voice inside urged him. "What can I lose?" he thought.

"Are you on marijuana, too? I know you drink. I can smell it on your breath." Josh felt relief. He had finally said it.

Pete turned red, but acted as if he didn't even hear it. "Wanna try one, Josh?" he coaxed, fingering the skinny cigarette. "These are great. We can smoke together, just you and me. Eldon smokes pot with his parents. Mom and Dad are too strict. We won't tell them. We'll blow the smoke out the window."

Josh was confused. He and Pete could be buddies again, sharing a secret. He could end this after-school misery simply by saying yes. Mom and Dad didn't have to know. But deep down, Josh knew better. He had learned about alcohol and other drugs in school. His teacher said that drugs fry your brain. Josh pictured a frying pan with Pete's brain in it, just like the commercial on TV. He imagined his mother carefully turning the pieces with a spatula. He shuddered.

"It's just one joint, Josh. Come on, we can be buddies again," Pete urged. He knew that Josh would not dare tell on him if they smoked the marijuana together.

"Do it," Josh's inner voice kept saying, "then you and Pete can be friends again."

"What do you think I am, an addict or something?" Pete asked, laughing.

Maybe it was the word addict. Or maybe it was Pete standing there red-eyed, hair mussed, dirty shirt, looking like he just got up. And it was 4:30 in the afternoon. Somehow, Josh knew that this was more than just an offer to smoke pot. He began to realize that his brother was desperate. In his imagination, Josh saw Old Lou, the neighborhood drunk, lying in the gutter behind Joe's bar, a bottle of Jack Daniels clutched in his arms. Only the face he saw wasn't Old Lou's, it was Pete's. Josh blinked and shook himself back to reality. Yes, Pete was desperate. He was in too deep to get out by himself.

"Come on, Josh. You don't believe all of the horror stories about drugs that the teachers ram down our throats, do you?"

Josh grabbed Pete's arm. "Listen to me. You've changed. I want things to be like they used to be. We had so much fun after school. Now you don't even notice me. But I won't take drugs. Please stop, Pete. Let's talk to Mom and Dad."

Pete pulled his arm from Josh's grasp. He was searching for a lighter in his pocket, barely listening. When he heard the words "talk to Mom and Dad," his voice rose in anger. "You tell them, you little creep, and you're in trouble. You're not my buddy. You're not even my brother. You're a coward." Pete turned his back and walked out of Josh's room.

Though he knew that he had made the right decision, Josh felt numb. His mind felt fuzzy. He needed to focus on one thing. "Mom's list. I need to start supper," he remembered.

Pete's face smiled down on him from the picture in the hallway as Josh headed toward the kitchen. "Life is strange sometimes," Josh thought. "I've always depended on Pete to help me. Now Pete needs my help. Tonight I'll tell Mom and Dad what happened. They'll know what to do."

Talk About the Story

If I were Josh, I would _____ .

Scripture

Sometimes we think that Jesus was never tempted. In today's story you will read how Jesus was tempted to forget that God was in charge of things. Read Luke 4:1–13.

A reading from the holy gospel according to Luke

When Jesus returned from the Jordan River, the power of the Holy Spirit was with him, and the Spirit led him into the desert. For forty days Jesus was tested by the devil, and during that time he went without eating. When it was all over, he was hungry.

The devil said to Jesus, "If you are God's Son, tell this stone to turn into bread."

Jesus answered, "The Scriptures say, 'No one can live only on food.' "

Then the devil led Jesus up to a high place and quickly showed him all the nations on earth. The devil said, "I will give all this power and glory to you. It has been given to me, and I can give it to anyone I want to. Just worship me, and you can have it all."

Jesus answered, "The Scriptures say: 'Worship the Lord your God and serve only him!' "

Finally, the devil took Jesus to Jerusalem and had him stand on top of the temple. The devil said, "If you are God's Son, jump off. The Scriptures say: 'God will tell his angels to take care of you. They will catch you in their arms, and you will not hurt your feet on the stones.' "

Jesus answered, "The Scriptures also say, 'Don't try to test the Lord your God!' "

After the devil had finished testing Jesus in every way possible, he left him for a while.

The gospel of the Lord.

Reflection

Jesus wanted God to be more important to us than food or anything else. How does our family celebrate God's importance?

Journal

See page 10, part 2 of your journal.

Prayer

God, our strength,
help us to build your kingdom on earth
with love and peace.
We place our petitions before you.

Our response will be: God is our strength.

Parent:	Help us to think of others' needs.
Response:	God is our strength.
Parent:	Help us to be kind and honest.
Response:	God is our strength.
Parent:	Help us to rely on your power rather than our own.
Response:	God is our strength.
Parent:	Together, let us say the prayer that Jesus gave us. Our Father, who art in heaven, hallowed be thy name; thy kingdom come; thy will be done on earth as it is in heaven. Give us this day our daily bread; and forgive us our trepasses as we forgive those who trespass against us;

and lead us not into temptation
but deliver us from evil.
Amen.

Blessing

Pour some vegetable oil or bath oil into a special container, and place it on the prayer table. Then bless each other's hands with the oil, saying:

(Name), may God strengthen you to be like Jesus. Amen.

Second Sunday of Lent

Jesus Is Changed

Based on Luke 9:28–36

Opening Question

Tell about a time when you changed your mind or your attitude about something. What happened that helped you change?

Journal

See page 11, part 1 of your journal.

Story

Today's story begins where last week's story ended. Remember Josh and his brother Pete? Josh felt sad when Pete was drinking alcohol and smoking marijuana. They were no longer friends. Today you will read a story of transformation, or change.

Pete and Me

Remember Me? I'm Josh. I know you're wondering what happened to Pete and me after I told him I wouldn't smoke pot.

I went to the kitchen to peel carrots for supper. That was the first thing on Mom's list. I was feeling sad and afraid that Pete and I could never be buddies again. But I knew I had to tell Mom and Dad that he was drinking and smoking pot.

I heard a car crunch the gravel in the driveway. It was only 5:30. Mom was home early. She looked surprised when she saw me. "Josh, what's the matter?" she said. I think she noticed I'd been crying. She motioned for me to sit down next to her at the kitchen table.

"Josh, what's wrong?" she asked again. "Pete should be helping with supper."

I couldn't stand it any longer. I knew Dad wouldn't be home for awhile, but I couldn't wait. I blurted out the whole story. Then I waited for Mom to scold me for not telling her about Pete's drinking sooner. But she didn't. She just took my hand and said, "Josh, I'm so sorry you had to go through this by yourself. You're not alone anymore. Dad and I will figure out what to do."

And they did. To make a long story short, Pete entered a treatment facility—I just learned that term—called Pine Sands. It's a place for teenagers to get help when they are addicted to alcohol and other drugs. Pete's been at Pine Sands three weeks now.

What I really want you to know is how Pete and I became friends again.

Yesterday, Pete's counselor, Mr. Graham, asked Mom and Dad to bring me along with them to the family program. I didn't really want to go because I was afraid Pete would yell at me again. My school counselor said she could understand why I didn't want to go. "If a dog keeps attacking you, you want to stay out of its way until it is tamed," she said. But Mom said it must be important if Mr. Graham asked me to come. So I decided to go.

Pine Sands was even bigger than my school. There were five buildings and a tennis court. The fence around it was friendly—I mean it was low enough to climb over. I thought I saw Pete hitting a tennis ball, and my heart jumped. But when the tennis player turned, I realized it was someone else.

We went in. A lady with frizzy red hair and long, dangly earrings looked over her glasses at Mom and Dad and me.

"Can I help you?" she asked.

"We're here to see Pete Carter," I said. The lady looked up a list of names on her desk, then picked up the phone and dialed a number. "Mr. Graham, your clients are here." She smiled at me. I felt important standing there in my blue Sunday jacket. I was a client.

My heart jumped again as Pete came around the corner. A short, blond man was with him. A scar on the man's cheek kept moving as he talked. "Hello, Mr. and Mrs. Carter. And you must be Josh."

Pete gave us each a hug. "Hi, buddy, I've sure missed you," he said to me. "Want to go for a walk?" Mr. Graham nodded, so I figured it must be okay. But I was nervous. Was he still mad at me for telling on him?

We walked along a gravel path, past a row of small brick buildings. "That's my cottage," Pete said as he pointed to a flat-roofed building. He explained that he lived there with nine other guys. "We do mostly everything there except eat our meals." He nudged me and said, "Hey, let's sit down so we can talk."

We found a bench nearby and sat in silence for a few moments. Then Pete said quietly, "Josh, I'm so glad you came. I know I hurt you. I am so sorry."

I wanted to tell him it was okay. But something held me back. I'd heard this stuff before. How could I trust that this time he meant it? And I knew we hadn't really settled what had happened that night he offered me the marijuana.

"Aren't you mad at me for telling Mom and Dad you were using drugs?"

"No, Josh, I'm glad you did. Because you told them, I'm getting the help I need. I was so blind. The alcohol changed me. I couldn't even think straight. And I never should have offered you that marijuana. I'm really sorry. I wouldn't blame you if you hated me."

I looked at Pete. His eyes were filled with tears. I couldn't hold my feelings in any longer.

"Pete, I don't hate you. I love you. You're my brother."

Pete smiled at me. "Josh, I'm so lucky to have you and Mom and Dad." His eyes were shining. I knew it wasn't just a smile to make me feel better. Pete was changed. This smile was coming from inside. I was sure Pete meant every word he was saying. But something else was bothering me.

"Pete, you won't drink again, will you? Promise me you won't."

Pete stopped smiling. "I wish I could promise you that, Josh. I know now that I'm alcoholic. That means I have a kind of allergy to alcohol—like you're allergic to milk. Alcohol makes me sick and mean, and if I start drinking, I can't stop. I can promise to ask God every day to help me not drink. I'll go to Alcoholics Anonymous meetings. My counselor says I have to stay sober, one day at a time."

I felt disappointed at first. I wanted Pete to say he'd never drink again. I'm still feeling kind of confused about everything Pete told me. Mom says I don't have to figure everything out at once. One thing I know for sure is that Pete has changed. He's happier than ever before. And he really cares about me. We're friends again.

Talk About the Story

Can you finish this sentence? If I were Josh, I _____ .

Scripture

Pete's face and attitude changed. He was transformed. Today's scripture, Luke 9:28–36, tells how Jesus was transformed.

> A reading from the holy gospel according to Luke
>
> Jesus took Peter, John, and James with him and went up on a mountain to pray. While he was praying, his face changed, and his clothes became shining white. Suddenly Moses and Elijah were there speaking with him. They appeared in heavenly glory and talked about all that Jesus' death in Jerusalem would mean.
>
> Peter and the other two disciples had been sound asleep. All at once they woke up and saw how glorious Jesus was. They also saw the two men who were with him.
>
> Moses and Elijah were about to leave, when Peter said to Jesus, "Master, it is good for us to be here! Let us make three shelters, one for you, one for Moses, and one for Elijah." But Peter did not know what he was talking about.
>
> While Peter was still speaking, a shadow from a cloud passed over them, and they were frightened as the cloud covered them. From the cloud a voice spoke, "This is my chosen Son. Listen to what he says!"
>
> After the voice had spoken, Peter, John, and James saw only Jesus. For some time they kept quiet and did not say anything about what they had seen.
>
> The gospel of the Lord.

Reflection

If you were with Jesus that day, what would you have seen? What would you have heard? How would you have felt?

Journal

See page 11, part 2 of your journal.

Prayer

Our prayer today will be a meditation. Close your eyes and relax. Take a few deep breaths.

Read in a slow, calm voice, pausing after each sentence.

In your mind, think of a beautiful place where you and Jesus can visit for awhile. Imagine a peaceful and quiet spot. You feel safe and relaxed.

Now you see Jesus coming close to you. Look at his face. Notice how happy he is to see you.

Jesus understands you. He loves you when you are peaceful and happy. But Jesus loves you when you are angry and crabby too. Jesus is your friend, no matter what.

Jesus truly understands your hidden feelings. He wants you to be happy. Feel Jesus put his arm around you. Listen to his voice. "I love you, *(child's name)*. I will give you my blessing now.

"We will always be friends. Remember, I am always with you." You feel Jesus' love and peace throughout your body. You are ready to radiate and shine goodness to all you meet.

Now open your eyes, and we will say the prayer that Jesus gave us.

Our Father, who art in heaven,
hallowed be thy name;
thy kingdom come;
thy will be done on earth
as it is in heaven.
Give us this day our daily bread;
and forgive us our trespasses
as we forgive those
who trespass against us;
and lead us not into temptation,
but deliver us from evil.
Amen.

In conclusion, give each other a hug or some sign of affection.

Third Sunday of Lent
God Gives Us Another Chance

Based on Luke 13:6 – 9

Opening Activity

Here is a simple game titled "Second Chance." It can be played with two or more people. Each player takes a turn guessing a letter. If the puzzle is not solved after one turn, then each player is given another chance until the puzzle is solved. Parent, see answer at the end of this session.

THE ___ ___ ___ ___ IS ___ ___ ___ ___

AND ___ ___ ___ ___ ___ ___ ___ ___ .

This might be a great traveling game or in-between-time game to be played with your child. You may want to take turns choosing familiar responsorial psalms, prayers or chapter titles from this book and set up puzzle sentences like the one above.

Discussion Question

Have you ever been given a second chance? Tell about it.

Scripture

Jesus talks about a second chance in today's scripture. Read Luke 13:6 – 9.

> A reading from the holy gospel according to Luke
>
> Jesus told the people this story:
> "A man had a fig tree growing in his vineyard. One day he went out to pick some figs, but he didn't find any. So he said to the gardener, 'For three years I have come looking for figs on this tree, and I haven't found any yet. Chop it down! Why should it take up space?'
> "The gardener answered, 'Master, leave it for another year. I'll dig around it and put some manure on it to make it grow. Maybe it will have figs on it next year. If it doesn't, you can have it cut down.'"
>
> The gospel of the Lord.

Reflection

If you were the fig tree, how would you have felt? What would you have said to the gardener?

Journal

See page 12 of your journal.

Prayer

Lord, you are kind and merciful,
slow to anger and full of love. *(Psalm 103:8)*
Giver of second chances,
help us to be patient and loving.
We ask this in Jesus' name. Amen.

Blessing

Cross your hands over your heart. Invite your child to do the same, saying "Let us pray quietly in our hearts." Then place your hands on the child's head, and say:

God, thank you for blessing *(Name)*
with kindness and love. Amen.

Answer to the Puzzle

The Lord is kind and merciful.

Fourth Sunday of Lent

God Always Forgives

Based on Luke 15:11–32

Opening Question

It is not always easy to forgive. Have you ever been able to forgive someone after that person hurt you? Tell about it.

Journal

See page 13, part 1 of your journal.

Story

Here is a play about forgiveness. Some people are able to forgive immediately; others have a hard time forgiving.

A Son Returns Home

Characters: Jacob, Jonathan, Mother, Father and Narrator

Narrator Scene one opens with a man peering down the road. He calls excitedly to his wife:

Father Come quick!
Look to the field!
Jonathan's back.
Thank God he wasn't killed.

Narrator The father and mother run to meet their son Jonathan.

Jonathan Father, Mother, forgive me
for gambling your savings away.
If you don't want me back,
I'll leave here today.

Narrator The parents hug their son, forgiving him immediately.

Parents Welcome back, Jonathan.
It's been such a long wait.
We'll have a big party.
We must celebrate.

Narrator But not everyone wants to celebrate. Jacob, Jonathan's older brother, is angry and jealous. He says to Jonathan:

Jacob You've got some nerve
coming back here
after spending Dad's money
on race cars and beer.

> I cant't believe
> he's letting you stay
> after all that you've done.
> Go on. Go away.

(Jacob turns to his parents and says)

> A party for him?
> You're not being fair.
> I've worked hard on the farm,
> but what do you care!

Parents
> You're our dear oldest son,
> of course we love you,
> but Jon left and came back.
> What else can we do?

Narrator
> So they partied past midnight
> as never before,
> with cake and ice cream
> and dancing galore.
> And they lived as a family,
> the oldest son, too.
> In his heart he loved Jonathan.
> What else could he do?

Talk About the Play

How would you have felt if you were Jacob, the older son?

Scripture

In Luke 15:11 – 32 you will find a story of forgiveness.

A reading from the holy gospel according to Luke

Then Jesus told them this story:

"Once a man had two sons. The younger son said to his father, 'Give me my share of the property.' So the father divided his property between his two sons.

"Not long after that, the younger son packed up everything he owned and left for a foreign country, where he wasted all his money in wild living. He had spent everything, when a bad famine spread through that whole land. Soon he had nothing to eat.

"He went to work for a man in that country, and the man sent him out to take care of his pigs. He would have been glad to eat what the pigs were eating, but no one gave him a thing.

"Finally, he came to his senses and said, 'My father's workers have plenty to eat, and here I am, starving to death! I will leave and go to my father and say to him, "Father, I have sinned against God in heaven and against you. I am no longer good enough to be called your son. Treat me like one of your workers." '

"The younger son got up and started back to his father. But when he was still a long way off, his father saw him and felt sorry for him. He ran to his son and hugged and kissed him.

"The son said, 'Father, I have sinned against God in heaven and against you. I am no longer good enough to be called your son.'

"But his father said to the servants, 'Hurry and bring the best clothes and put them on him. Give him a ring for his finger and sandals for his feet. Get the best calf and prepare it, so we can eat and celebrate. This son of mine was dead, but has now come back to life. He was lost and has now been found.' And they began to celebrate."

The gospel of the Lord.

Reflection

What would it have been like to be the son that returned home? What would it have been like to be his parents?

Journal

See page 13, part 2 of your journal.

Prayer

Loving God, your Son Jesus forgave his enemies
as he hung on the cross.
Forgive us our sins
as we forgive those who sin against us.
We ask this in Jesus' name. Amen.

Blessing

Give each other a sign of peace, saying:

May the peace of Christ be with you.

Fifth Sunday of Lent

God Sets Us Free

Based on John 8:1–11

Opening Question

Have you ever felt trapped? What made you feel that way? What happened?

Story

Here is a story about a girl who felt trapped by what her friends thought about her.

The Pocket Watch

Except for an occasional cough or the scratching of a pencil on paper, the room was as quiet as the snow that was falling gently outside the school window. Margo finished the English test and sat staring at the pocket watch on the edge of Mr. Badler's desk. The gold chain sparkled in the sunlight. She was thinking, "If I had the money, I'd buy my father a watch like that."

Margo's stomach tightened when she thought of what happened last night. She and Duane were drying dishes. Margo flicked the dish towel at her brother, teasing him, but she missed and knocked her dad's watch from the sink ledge into the garbage disposal. Crunch, crunch, she heard. Both the watch and garbage disposal were broken.

"Time's up," Mr. Badler called, taking off his jacket and hanging it over the back of the chair. "Mm-mmm" he said. "Do I smell pizza? It must be time for lunch. I'll see you back here at 12:30 for the geography test."

If Margo had known what would happen next, she would have hurried from the room like the rest of the class. Instead, she stopped to sharpen her pencil. As she passed Mr. Badler's desk, she noticed the half-open drawer. There was the watch. Leaning close, she could see the likeness of a deer on the gold case. She ran her fingers over the delicate etching. "Oh, how Dad would love a watch like this." She lifted it to the light looking for a brand name. She opened and closed the case. Dangling the gold chain this way and that, Margo eyed the elegant timepiece from every angle, as if she were an expert watch dealer inspecting a new purchase.

Then she slipped it into her sweater pocket. But when she tried to pull the watch out again, the chain got caught on a loose piece of yarn.

"Oh, no," she cried as she desperately tried to untangle the chain.

Just then, Marilyn Morris ran back into the room to get her comb. When she saw Margo with Mr. Badler's watch in her pocket, she quickly turned and disappeared down the hall.

Minutes later, Marilyn returned with Mr. Badler. "See, she still has it!" she said. Mr. Badler told Marilyn to go back to the lunchroom.

"What are you doing with my watch?" Mr. Badler demanded, his face growing a deep shade of red. Margo felt trapped. Her mouth was dry, and she trembled as she faced Mr. Badler's anger. "I wasn't going to keep it," she managed to stammer. "Last night I broke my dad's watch. I was just checking your watch for the brand name when it got tangled up on my sweater."

Mr. Badler found this hard to believe until Margo showed him the chain tangled around the yarn. For a few moments he didn't say a word.

"Margo, I believe you," he finally said. "You have never lied to me. But it was wrong of you to meddle with my property without asking me first. Let's get this chain untangled before the rest of the class gets back from lunch." But it was too late.

Some of the children were already coming into the room, whispering and pointing at Margo.

"Margo's a thief," someone said. "Margo's a thief," others echoed. Marilyn must have told the whole class what she had seen. Kim, Bobby Joe, Cicely, Heather — even Nell, one of her best friends, stayed away from her.

"I am not a thief," Margo insisted. "I wasn't going to keep it."

She heard someone snicker, "She wasn't going to keep it. Hey, Margo, what was it doing in your pocket?"

A large paper dart flew through the air and landed on her desk. "Let's get the thief," someone yelled.

Margo felt ashamed and could bear no more. Why was no one defending her? She put her hands over her ears and laid her head on the desk.

Mr. Badler surveyed the chaos around him, then riveted his eyes on each person in turn. He raised his arms for silence. The group quieted down.

"I believe you, Margo," he said loudly. Then he turned to the class, "Is there anyone here who has not made a mistake, never done anything wrong?"

Two hands crept up. "I mean in your whole entire life." The hands went down.

"If there is someone here who has never hurt another person, speak up now or leave Margo alone."

No one spoke. The room was so quiet you could hear the ticking of the pocket watch in Mr. Badler's hand.

"All right then, class, take out your paper and pencils for the geography test. I'll leave my watch here on your desk, Margo. Let me know when it's two o'clock. Class, you may begin."

With that Mr. Badler sat down in his chair, pulled a book from his desk drawer and began to read.

Talk About the Story

Margo felt trapped in this story. If you were one of Margo's classmates, how could you have helped her to be free and happy again?

Scripture

Read John 8:1–11 and see how Jesus sets someone free.

A reading from the holy gospel according to John

Jesus spent the night on the Mount of Olives. Then early the next morning he went to the temple. The people came to him, and he sat down and started teaching them.

The Pharisees and the teachers of the Law of Moses brought in a woman who had been caught in bed with a man who was not her husband. They made her stand in the middle of the crowd. Then they said, "Teacher, this woman was caught sleeping with a man who is not her husband. The Law of Moses teaches that a woman like this should be stoned to death! What do you say?"

They asked Jesus this question, because they wanted to test him and bring some charge against him. But Jesus simply bent over and started writing on the ground with his finger.

The crowd kept on asking Jesus about the woman. Finally, he stood up and said, "If any of you have never sinned, then go ahead and throw the first stone at her!" Once again he bent over and began writing on the ground. The people left one by one, beginning with the oldest one in the crowd. Finally, Jesus and the woman were there alone.

    Jesus stood up and asked her, "Where is everyone? Isn't there anyone left to accuse you?"

    "No, sir," the woman answered.

    Then Jesus told her, "I am not going to accuse you either. You may go now, but don't sin anymore."

The gospel of the Lord.

Reflection

If you were in the crowd, what would you have noticed about Jesus in this story? Is there any situation in your life where you would like to be treated more kindly or where you could treat someone else more kindly?

Journal

See page 14 of your journal.

Prayer

Gentle God,
you want us to be free
so we can be loving and happy.
Help us to use our freedom
to set others free
by our kind words and actions.
We ask this in Jesus' name. Amen.

Blessing

Bless each other by making a large sign of the cross over one another while saying:

(Name), **God's love sets you free.**

Passion Sunday

(Palm Sunday)

Based on Luke 19:28 – 40

Christians set aside an entire week to meditate on the great gift of love that Jesus gave us. The gift of his death and resurrection saved us from darkness and sin. Holy Week starts with Passion Sunday, which is often known as Palm Sunday, when we remember Jesus' triumphant entry into Jerusalem. When you go to Mass this Sunday, be sure to pick up palms at the church entrance and bring them to your home. Many Catholics put the palms they get today in a special place, often tucked behind a religious picture or a cross on the wall. Sometimes people weave their palms into the shape of a cross. You may wish to put your palms on the prayer table.

Scripture

In today's reading, Jesus is honored as a king. Read Luke 19:28 – 40 and imagine that you are there with Jesus.

> A reading from the holy gospel according to Luke
>
> Jesus went toward Jerusalem. As he was getting near to Bethphage and Bethany on the Mount of Olives, he sent two of his disciples on ahead. He told them, "Go into the next village, where you will find a young donkey that has never been ridden. Untie the donkey and bring it here. If anyone asks you why you are doing that, just say, 'The Lord needs it.' "
>
> They went off and found everything just as Jesus had said. While they were untying the donkey, its owners asked, "Why are you doing that?"
>
> They answered, "The Lord needs it."
>
> Then they led the donkey to Jesus. They put some of their clothes on its back and helped Jesus get on. And as he rode along, the people spread clothes on the road in front of him. When Jesus was starting down the Mount of Olives, his large crowd of disciples were happy and praised God because of all the miracles they had seen. They shouted, "Blessed is the king who comes in the name of the Lord! Peace in heaven and glory to God."
>
> Some Pharisees in the crowd said to Jesus, "Teacher, make your disciples stop shouting!"
>
> But Jesus answered, "If they keep quiet, these stones will start shouting."
>
> The gospel of the Lord.

Reflection

If you had been in the crowd that day, what would you have seen? done? heard? thought?

Journal

See page 15 of your journal.

Prayer

Have each person read the prayers that they wrote in their journals, or, holding up the palms from Sunday's liturgy, use the following prayer.

Loving God, we praise you.
We thank you. We ask your blessings.
Hosannah in the highest!
Thank you for sending us Jesus
to show us how you want us to live.
Blessed is he who comes in the name of the Lord,
now and forever!
Amen.

Blessing

Make the sign of the cross or touch each person on the forehead, saying:

May you be blessed, in the name of the Father, and of the Son, and of the Holy Spirit. Amen.

Triduum

On Holy Thursday, Lent is finished. The Mass of the Lord's Supper, celebrated on Holy Thursday evening, begins a three-day celebration called the Easter Triduum (triduum means "three days"). Christians throughout the world remember the Lord's Last Supper and his commands to serve each other and to remember him in the breaking of the bread, the eucharist.

On Good Friday, we recall the glory of Jesus' passion and death. Because we know that the story of Jesus' death does not end at the cross, we hear this story with faith in the resurrection.

During the day on Holy Saturday, many parishes have special gatherings for those who will be baptized or received into the Catholic church at the Easter Vigil that evening.

The Easter Vigil is the most important celebration in the church year. We rejoice that through the death and resurrection of Jesus we have meaning for our daily lives. Also, this night is extra special because the church welcomes new members at this liturgy through baptism.

Participating in the Holy Thursday and Good Friday liturgies with the community will best prepare your child for the Easter Vigil. However, if you are unable to attend, use the following three Bible stories to prepare your child for the biggest feast of the church. One story can be read on Holy Thursday, one on Good Friday, and the last one on Holy Saturday.

HOLY THURSDAY

Activity

With your child, make or buy grape juice and a loaf of bread that can be broken.

Scripture

The Gospel of John tells the story of how Jesus was the servant of all and expected his disciples also to serve. This reading is from John 13:3–17.

> A reading from the holy gospel according to John
>
> Jesus knew that he had come from God and would go back to God. He also knew that the Father had given him complete power. So during the meal Jesus got up, removed his outer garment, and wrapped a towel around his waist. He put some water into a large bowl. Then he began washing his disciples' feet and drying them with the towel he was wearing.
>
> But when he came to Simon Peter, that disciple asked, "Lord, are you going to wash my feet?"
> Jesus answered, "You don't really know what I am doing, but later you will understand."
> "You will never wash my feet!" Peter repliled.
> "If I don't wash you," Jesus told him, "you don't really belong to me."
> Peter said, "Lord, don't wash just my feet. Wash my hands and my head."
> Jesus answered, "People who have bathed and are clean all over need to wash just their feet. And you, my disciples, are clean, except for one of you."
> Jesus knew who would betray him. That is why he said, "except for one of you."
> After Jesus washed his disciples' feet and had put his outer garment back on, he sat down again. Then he said:
> "Do you understand what I have done? You call me your teacher and Lord, and you should, because that is who I am. And if your Lord and teacher has washed your feet, you should do the same for each other. I have set the example, and you should do for each other exactly what I have done for you. I tell you for certain that servants are not greater than their master, and messengers are not greater than the one who sent them. You know these things, and God will bless you, if you do them."
>
> The gospel of the Lord.

Journal

See page 16 of your journal.

Meal Prayer

Place both the bread and the grape juice in the center of the table. Then read this passage (Luke 22:19–20):

Jesus took some bread in his hands and gave thanks for it. He broke the bread and handed it to his apostles. Then he said, "This is my body, which is given for you. Eat this as a way of remembering me!"

After the meal he took a cup of wine in his hands. Then he said, "This is my blood. It is poured out for you, and with it God makes his new agreement."

After each person has had some bread and grape juice, continue with the meal.

Good Friday

Scripture

Today is Good Friday. We celebrate that Jesus saved us when he died on the cross. It is a day of both sadness and joy. We read the story of Jesus' death from the Gospel of Luke (22:39 — 23:56).

A reading from the holy gospel according to Luke

Jesus went out to the Mount of Olives, as he often did, and his disciples went with him. When they got there, he told them, "Pray that you will not be tested."

Jesus walked on a little way before he kneeled down and prayed, "Father, if you will, please don't make me suffer by having me drink from this cup. But do what you want, and not what I want."

Then an angel from heaven came to help him. Jesus was in great pain and prayed so sincerely that his sweat fell to the ground like drops of blood.

Jesus got up from praying and went over to his disciples. They were asleep and worn out from being so sad. He said to them, "Why are you asleep? Wake up and pray that you will not be tested."

While Jesus was still speaking, a crowd came up. It was led by Judas, one of the twelve apostles. He went over to Jesus and greeted him with a kiss.

Jesus asked Judas, "Are you betraying the Son of Man with a kiss?"

When Jesus' disciples saw what was about to happen, they asked, "Lord, should we attack them with a sword?" One of the disciples even struck at the high priest's servant with his sword and cut off the servant's right ear.

"Enough of that!" Jesus said. Then he touched the servant's ear and healed it.

Jesus spoke to the chief priests, the temple police, and the leaders who had come to arrest him. He said, "Why do you come out with swords and clubs and treat me like a criminal? I was with you everyday in the temple, and you didn't arrest me. But this is your time, and darkness is in control."

Jesus was arrested and led away to the house of the high priest, while Peter followed at a distance. Some people built a fire in the middle of the courtyard and were sitting around it. Peter sat there with them, and a servant girl saw him. Then after she had looked at him carefully, she said, "This man was with Jesus!"

Peter said, "Woman, I don't even know that man!"

A little later someone else saw Peter and said, "You surely are one of them!"

"No, I'm not!" Peter replied.

About an hour later another man insisted, "This man must have been with Jesus. They both come from Galilee."

Peter replied, "I don't know what you are talking about!" Right then, while Peter was still speaking, a rooster crowed.

The Lord turned and looked at Peter. And Peter remembered that the Lord had said, "Before a rooster crows tomorrow morning, you will say three times that you don't know me." Then Peter went out and cried hard.

The men who were guarding Jesus made fun of him and beat him. They put a blindfold on him and said, "Tell us who struck you!" They kept on insulting Jesus in many other ways.

At daybreak the nation's leaders, the chief priests, and the teachers of the Law of Moses got together and brought Jesus before their council. They said, "Tell us! Are you the Messiah?"

Jesus replied, "If I said so, you wouldn't believe me. And if I asked you a question, you wouldn't answer. But from now on the Son of Man will be seated at the right side of God All-Powerful."

Then they asked, "Are you the Son of God?"

Jesus answered, "You say I am!"

They replied, "Why do we need more witnesses? He said it himself!"

Everyone in the council got up and led Jesus off to Pilate. They started accusing him and said, "We caught this man trying to get our people to riot and to stop paying taxes to the Emperor. He also claims that he is the Messiah, our king."

Pilate asked Jesus, "Are you the king of the Jews?"

"Those are your words," Jesus answered.

Pilate told the chief priests and the crowd, "I don't find him guilty of anything."

But they all kept on saying, "He has been teaching and causing trouble all over Judea. He started in Galilee and has now come all the way here."

When Pilate heard this, he asked, "Is this man from Galilee?" After Pilate learned that Jesus came from the region ruled by Herod, he sent him to Herod, who was in Jerusalem at that time.

For a long time Herod had wanted to see Jesus and was very happy because he finally had this chance. He had heard many things about Jesus and hoped to see him work a miracle.

Herod asked him a lot of questions, but Jesus did not answer. Then the chief priests and the teachers of the Law of Moses stood up and accused him of all kinds of bad things.

Herod and his soldiers made fun of Jesus and insulted him. They put a fine robe on him and sent him back to Pilate. That same day Herod and Pilate became friends, even though they had been enemies before this.

Pilate called together the chief priests, the leaders, and the people. He told them, "You brought Jesus to me and said he was a troublemaker. But I have questioned him here in front of you, and I have not found him guilty of anything that you say he has done. Herod didn't find him guilty either and sent him back. This man doesn't deserve to be put to death! I will just have him beaten with a whip and set free."

But the whole crowd shouted, "Kill Jesus! Give us Barabbas!" Now Barabbas was in jail because he had started a riot in the city and had murdered someone.

Pilate wanted to set Jesus free, so he spoke again to the crowds. But they kept shouting, "Nail him to a cross! Nail him to a cross!"

Pilate spoke to them a third time, "But what crime has he done? I have not found him guilty of anything for which he should be put to death. I will have him beaten with a whip and set free."

The people kept on shouting as loud as they could for Jesus to be put to death. Finally, Pilate gave in. He freed the man who was in jail for rioting and murder, because he was the one the crowd wanted to be set free. Then Pilate handed Jesus over for them to do what they wanted with him.

As Jesus was being led away, some soldiers grabbed hold of a man from Cyrene named Simon. He was coming in from the fields, but they put the cross on him and made him carry it behind Jesus.

A large crowd was following Jesus, and in the crowd a lot of women were crying and weeping for him. Jesus turned to the women and said:

> Women of Jerusalem, don't cry for me! Cry for yourselves and for your children. Someday people will say, "Women who never had children are really fortunate!" At that time everyone will say to the mountains, "Fall on us!" They will say to the hills, "Hide us!" If this can happen when the wood is green, what do you think will happen when it is dry?

Two criminals were led out to be put to death with Jesus. When the soldiers came to the place called "The Skull," they nailed Jesus to a cross. They also nailed the two criminals to two crosses, one on each side of Jesus.

Jesus said, "Father, forgive these people! They don't know what they're doing."

While the crowd stood there watching Jesus, the soldiers gambled for his clothes. The leaders insulted him by saying, "He saved others. Now he should save himself if he really is God's chosen Messiah."

The soldiers made fun of Jesus and brought him some wine. They said, "If you are the king of the Jews, save yourself!"

Above him was a sign that said, "This is the King of the Jews."

One of the criminals hanging there also insulted Jesus by saying, "Aren't you the Messiah? Save yourself and save us!"

But the other criminal told the first one off, "Don't you fear God? Aren't you getting the same punishment as this man? We got what was coming to us, but he didn't do anything wrong." Then he said to Jesus, "Remember me when you come into power!"

Jesus replied, "I promise that today you will be with me in paradise."

Around noon the sky turned dark and stayed that way until the middle of the afternoon. The sun stopped shining, and the curtain in the temple split down the middle. Jesus shouted, "Father I put myself in your hands!" Then he died.

When the Roman officer saw what had happened, he praised God and said, "Jesus must really have been a good man!"

A crowd had gathered to see the terrible sight. After they saw it, they felt brokenhearted and went home. All of Jesus' close friends and the women who had come with him from Galilee stood at a distance and watched.

There was a man named Joseph, who was from Arimathea in Judea. Joseph was a good and honest man, and he was eager for God's kingdom to come. He was also a member of the Jewish council, but he did not agree with what they had decided.

Joseph went to Pilate and asked for Jesus' body. He took the body down from the cross and wrapped it in fine cloth. Then he put it in a tomb that had been cut out of solid rock and had never been used. It was Friday, and the Sabbath was about to begin.

The women who had come with Jesus' body saw him placed in the tomb. Then they went to prepare some sweet-smelling spices for his burial. But on the Sabbath they rested, as the Law of Moses commands.

The gospel of the Lord.

Reflection

Spend some time together quietly thinking about the scripture and writing in your journal on page 17.

Optional Activity

(Also found in child's journal) If you and your child have not made a resurrection cross, you may want to do this activity together. Cut cardboard in the shape of a cross. Decorate it with colorful stones, old jewelry, tissue paper, spray-painted noodles or any material that is shiny and beautiful. When finished, place it on the prayer table.

Prayer and Blessing

Cover the prayer table with a red or purple cloth. On it, place a cross, a crucifix or the resurrection cross your child made earlier. You may want to add some palms from last Sunday. Invite your child to hold up the cross while you pray:

**We adore you, O Christ, and we thank you,
for by your holy cross you have saved the world.**

Then have everyone take the cross and form a large sign of the cross over each other's entire body, saying:

(Name), **by the cross of Jesus you are saved, in the name of the Father, and of the Son, and of the Holy Spirit. Amen.**

Holy Saturday

Activity

Color Easter eggs together. Explain that the egg is a symbol of Jesus' resurrection. The egg is the tomb, and when the chick hatches, it symbolizes Jesus' new life on Easter morning. You may want to read the following scripture selection.

Scripture

Paul's letter to the Philippians (the Christians who lived in the city of Philippi) tells us that we should imitate Jesus' humility and love. This reading is from Philippians 2:1 – 11.

A reading from the letter to the Philippians

Christ encourages you, and his love comforts you. God's Spirit unites you and you are concerned for others. Now make me completely happy! Live in harmony by showing love for each other. Be united in what you think, as if you were only one person. Don't be jealous or proud, but be humble and consider others more important than yourselves. Care about them as much as you care about yourselves and think the same way that Christ Jesus did.

> Christ was truly God.
> But he did not try to remain
>   equal with God.
> He gave up everything
>   and became a slave,
> when he became
>   like one of us.
>
> Christ was humble.
> He obeyed God and even died
>   on a cross.
> Then God gave Christ
>   the highest place
> and honored his name
>   above all others.
>
> So at the name of Jesus
>   everyone will bow down,
> those in heaven, on earth,
>   and under the earth.
> And to the glory
>   of God the Father
> everyone will openly agree,
>   "Jesus Christ is Lord!"

The word of the Lord

Easter Season

The joy of Jesus' resurrection is too great to last just one day! Easter is a season of fifty days, a week of weeks—seven times seven days plus one!

How do you celebrate for fifty days? You can't keep Easter eggs that long. And lilies get pretty droopy after a couple of weeks.

But you can keep a pretty bowl of fresh water on the dinner table or on the prayer table to remind you of your baptism. Sing an Alleluia when you pray before meals. Decorate a special candle and light it during meals or at prayer times. Bring fresh flowers to someone who would love them—and keep a few for yourself. If you live in a place where cold weather is giving way to spring, be sure to notice new buds and tender leaves.

Many Easter customs revolve around special foods. People love rich, sweet things after a long fast, and beautiful, green things after a long winter. Find out about Easter customs and foods around the world from people in your parish or books at the library.

Easter

Alleluia, Jesus Lives

Based on Luke 24:1 – 12

Opening Activity

Our Easter traditions provide many symbols of resurrection or new life. Choose an activity that best fits your family situation.

- Put Christian symbols on Easter eggs (for example, a cross, a rising sun, water, a candle, bread and wine).
- Have an Easter egg hunt.
- Prepare an Easter basket for someone.
- Get up early on Easter morning and watch the sun rise out of the darkness. Discuss how the sunrise symbolizes Jesus rising out of the tomb.
- If you have a new Easter outfit, talk about how it is a symbol of new life.
- Buy an Easter lily that is ready to bloom, and watch how the flower bursts out of the bud.
- Watch for butterflies in the coming weeks and talk about new life or transformed life coming from a caterpillar, chrysalis or cocoon.
- Discover together the Easter symbols in the church today.
- Decorate a large candle with a cross, water, flowers or other symbols of new life. Use the candle throughout the 50 days of Easter.

Scripture

Jesus springs a surprise on his friends and, when you think of it, the whole world.
Read Luke 24:1 – 12 and see what Jesus did.

> **A reading from the holy gospel according to Luke**
>
> Very early on Sunday morning the women went to the tomb, carrying the spices that they had prepared. When they found the stone rolled away from the entrance, they went in. But they did not find the body of the Lord Jesus, and they did not know what to think.
>
> Suddenly two men in shining white clothes stood beside them. The women were afraid and bowed to the ground. But the men said, "Why are you looking in the place of the dead for someone who is alive? Jesus is not here! He has been raised from death. Remember that while he was still in Galilee, he told you, 'The Son of Man will be handed over to sinners who will nail him to a cross. But three days later he will rise to life.'"
>
> Mary Magdalene, Joanna, Mary the mother of James, and some other women were the ones who had gone to the tomb. When they returned, they told the eleven apostles and the others what had happened. The apostles thought it was all nonsense, and they would not believe.
>
> But Peter ran to the tomb. And when he stooped down and looked in, he saw only the burial clothes. Then he returned, wondering what had happened.
>
> **The gospel of the Lord.**

Reflection

Imagine that you are standing at the empty tomb. What would surprise you?

Journal

See page 18 of your journal.

Prayer

Drape a colorful cloth on the prayer table. Place symbols of new life on the cloth. Then share your journal prayers or the following:

This is the day the Lord has made
let us rejoice and be glad in it. *(Psalm 118:24)*
God, giver of life,
we praise and thank you
in the name of Jesus,
who rose on this Easter day.
Alleluia!

Blessing

Share a hug or a kiss, or both, and say:

Alleluia! Jesus lives. And he lives in you.

Second Sunday of Easter
We Believe!

Based on John 20:19–31

Opening Activity

Faith is a gift from God. Here is a play about Thomas, one of the apostles. He had trouble believing that Jesus had risen from the dead. If your family is small, each person may need to take more than one part. There are six characters: Narrator, Jesus, Thomas, Disciple 1, Disciple 2 and Disciple 3.

The Big Surprise

Act 1

Narrator	Act one opens with the disciples quietly hiding in the upper room for fear of Jesus' enemies. They are grieving because Jesus died on the cross three days ago. They miss their teacher and friend very much. Just this morning, however, Mary Magdalene told them that Jesus appeared to her.
Disciple 1	Did someone lock the door after Thomas left this afternoon? *(Everyone shakes their head "no.")* We've got to be careful. The enemies of Jesus might come after us now. Let's remember to keep this locked. *(Gets up to check the door)*
Disciple 2	Do you think Mary really saw Jesus?
Disciple 1	I don't know, she was crying a lot yesterday. Maybe she's imagining things.
Jesus	*(Enters the room quietly)*
Disciple 3	*(Gasps in surprise)* It's Jesus! He's alive!
Jesus	*(Smiles)* Peace be with you. Yes, it is really I. See my hands where they put the nails?
All	*(Kneel and look surprised.)*
Jesus	*(Breathes deeply and spreads his hands over the entire group)* Peace be with you. As God sent me to you, I now send you to tell the good news to others. Receive the Holy Spirit. If you forgive people's sins, they are forgiven. If you do not forgive, they will never be at complete peace. I will leave you now for awhile, but you will see me again. Shalom.

Act 2

Narrator	Act two. Jesus left that night. The disciples are very surprised and confused. Thomas, who was absent, now returns to the upper room.
Disciple 1	Thomas, check the door to make sure it is locked. We do not want the enemies of Jesus to attack us. You'll never believe who came to visit while you were gone.
Thomas	*(While Thomas checks the door, he says)* Who was here?
Disciple 2	Jesus came. He showed us the wounds in his hands.
Thomas	I'll never believe that without putting my fingers into those wounds and my hand into his side where they pierced his heart.

Act 3

Narrator   Act three opens a week later. Thomas has been miserable all week. Could it be true that his friends saw Jesus? How was that possible? Jesus is dead! All the disciples are present in the upper room. The doors are securely locked, and Jesus appears.

Jesus   Peace be with you. *(Looking at Thomas)* Hello, Thomas, I missed you last Sunday. You had a hard time believing that I visited our friends here. Come now. See my hands? Put your finger into them. It doesn't hurt. Give me your hand. Place it into my side. Believe that I am alive.

Narrator   Thomas is surprised to see Jesus and is even more surprised by what he says. Thomas lets Jesus take his hand and place it into the wounds.

Thomas   *(Falls to his knees)* My Lord and my God.

Jesus   Thomas, my friend, you believe because you have seen me. Blessed are all those who have not seen me but believe.

Narrator   Thomas was now a believer. But all of you *(looking at the group)* are holy because you believe that Jesus is your Lord and God.

Talk About the Play

Imagine that you are the character you played. How would you feel?

Scripture

The play is based on the story found in the Gospel of John (20:19–29). Imagine that you are there with Jesus.

A reading from the holy gospel according to John

The disciples were afraid of the Jewish leaders, and on the evening of that same Sunday they locked themselves in a room. Suddenly, Jesus appeared in the middle of the group. He greeted them and showed them his hands and his side. When the disciples saw the Lord, they became very happy.

After Jesus had greeted them again, he said, "I am sending you, just as the Father has sent me." Then he breathed on them and said, "Receive the Holy Spirit. If you forgive anyone's sins, they will be forgiven. But if you don't forgive their sins, they will not be forgiven."

Although Thomas the Twin was one of the twelve disciples, he was not with the others when Jesus appeared to them. So they told him, "We have seen the Lord!"

But Thomas said, "First, I must see the nail scars in his hands and touch them with my finger. I must put my hand where the spear went into his side. I won't believe unless I do this!"

A week later the disciples were together again. This time Thomas was with them. Jesus came in while the doors were still locked and stood in the middle of the group. He greeted his disciples and said to Thomas, "Put your finger here and look at my hands! Put your hand into my side. Stop doubting and have faith!"

Thomas replied, "You are my Lord and my God!"

Jesus said, "Thomas, do you have faith because you have seen me? The people who have faith in me without seeing me are the ones who are really blessed!"

The gospel of the Lord.

Reflection

How do you show that you believe in Jesus?

Activity

When you go to Sunday Mass this week, you may want to bring a small bottle with you to take some blessed Easter water home. This holy water could be used at your family prayer and blessing.

Journal

See page 19 of your journal.

Prayer

Place a Bible and a lighted candle on the prayer table. Invite each person to take turns reading a faith statement about Jesus from their journal. After each statement, respond with "My Lord and my God." Or pray the Apostles' Creed together. You might read the Creed in short segments and invite everyone to respond to each segment with the same response.

I believe in God, the Father almighty,
> creator of heaven and earth.

I believe in Jesus Christ, his only Son, our Lord.
> He was conceived by the power of the Holy Spirit
>> and born of the Virgin Mary.
>
> He suffered under Pontius Pilate,
>> was crucified, died and was buried.
>
> He descended to the dead.
> On the third day he rose again.
> He ascended into heaven,
>> and is seated at the right hand of the Father.
>
> He will come again to judge the living and the dead.

I believe in the Holy Spirit,
> the holy catholic Church,
> the communion of saints,
> the forgiveness of sins,
> the resurrection of the body,
> and the life everlasting.
> Amen.

Blessing

Bless each other on the forehead, saying:

My Lord and my God, deepen *(Name)*'s faith.

Third Sunday of Easter

Recognizing Jesus

Based on John 21:1–14

Opening Activity

Choose one of the following:

1. Look through some old family photos and have your child try to identify who is who. Ask, "Can you recognize (name) in this picture?"
2. Play the "I Recognize You" game. One person volunteers to be "it." "It" is blindfolded or leaves the room. The others in the room take turns calling "it's" name with disguised voices. "It" tries to guess who called by saying, "I recognized (name)'s voice."
3. Tell about a time when you did not recognize someone right away.

Scripture

After his resurrection, Jesus often appeared to his disciples. Sometimes they did not recognize him. In your imagination, join the disciples on a fishing trip and see what happens. Read John 21:1–14.

> A reading from the holy gospel according to John
>
> Jesus later appeared to his disciples along the shore of Lake Tiberias. Simon Peter, Thomas the Twin, Nathanael from Cana in Galilee, and the two sons of Zebedee, were there, together with two other disciples. Simon Peter said, "I'm going fishing!"
>
> The others said, "We'll go with you." They went out in their boat. But they didn't catch a thing that night.
>
> Early the next morning Jesus stood on the shore, but the disciples did not realize who he was. Jesus shouted, "Friends, have you caught anything?"
>
> "No!" they answered.
>
> So he told them, "Let your net down on the right side of your boat, and you will catch some fish."
>
> They did, and the net was so full of fish that they could not drag it up into the boat.
>
> Jesus' favorite disciple told Peter, "It's the Lord!" When Simon heard that it was the Lord, he put on the clothes that he had taken off while he was working. Then he jumped into the water. The boat was only about a hundred yards from shore. So the other disciples stayed in the boat and dragged in the net full of fish.
>
> When the disciples got out of the boat, they saw some bread and a charcoal fire with fish on it. Jesus told his disciples, "Bring some of the fish you just caught." Simon Peter got back into the boat and dragged the net to shore. In it were one hundred fifty-three large fish, but still the net did not rip.
>
> Jesus said, "Come and eat!" But none of the disciples dared ask who he was. They knew he was the Lord. Jesus took the bread in his hands and gave some of it to his disciples. He did the same with the fish.
>
> This was the third time that Jesus appeared to his disciples after he was raised from death.
>
> **The gospel of the Lord.**

Reflection

If you were in the boat with the disciples, what things would you have seen? What would it be like to have breakfast with Jesus?

Journal

See page 20 of your journal.

Prayer

If possible, gather for prayer in the kitchen or dining room. Have a container of holy water nearby.

Jesus,
your disciples recognized you
when you made breakfast for them.
Help us to recognize your presence
in the ordinary things of life,
especially when we share a meal together.

Blessing

Sprinkle the table and each other with holy water, and say:

Holy God,
bless our family.
May we recognize your love in each other
each time we gather around this table.
We ask this in Jesus' name. Amen.

Fourth Sunday of Easter

Jesus, the Good Shepherd

Based on John 10:27–30

Opening Question

Who do you want to take care of you when you are sick or hurting? Tell what you like about this person.

Journal

See page 21, part 1 of your journal.

Scripture

Today's scripture tells us how Jesus compares himself to a shepherd who cares for his flock. Read John 10:27–30.

> A reading from the holy gospel according to John
>
> Jesus said to his disciples: "My sheep know my voice, and I know them. They follow me, and I give them eternal life, so that they will never be lost. No one can snatch them out of my hand. My Father gave them to me, and he is greater than all others. No one can snatch them from his hands, and I am one with the Father."
>
> The gospel of the Lord.

Reflection

What did you hear in the reading? Imagine you are sick or need help, and Jesus is caring for you. What would that be like?

Journal

See page 21, part 2 of your journal.

Prayer

Today's prayer is a meditation. To begin, encourage your child to sit in a comfortable position. Read in a slow, calm voice. Give your child plenty of time to follow your directions.

Close your eyes. Quiet yourself. Relax. *(Pause)*

Take a few deep breaths. Breathe in through your nose. Now slowly let the air out from your mouth. *(Repeat these instructions a few times. When the child is relaxed, continue.)*

Feel the peace and quiet of a beautiful day. See yourself enjoying God's wonderful world around you. You are in one of your favorite places. Look around. Where are you? What do you see?

Then, what a great surprise! Jesus is coming toward you. He wants to spend some time with just you. He gives you a big smile. His eyes are filled with love and warmth. You know that he likes you very much. You two are good friends. You laugh together.

What would you like to say to Jesus? *(Pause 10 seconds.)*

What is Jesus saying to you? *(Pause 10 seconds.)*

Jesus puts his arm around your shoulder, like friends often do. He loves you. Jesus cares for you.

Tell Jesus how you feel about him. Thank him for his love and protection. *(Pause 10 seconds.)*

When you are ready, open your eyes.

Blessing

Place your hands on each other's head or shoulders, or give another sign of affection, saying:
May Jesus, the Good Shepherd, bless you.

Fifth Sunday of Easter

Love One Another

John 13:31–35

Opening Question

How would you know the difference between a genuine dollar bill and a counterfeit one? How would you tell the difference between a real flower and a silk flower?

Story

Here is a story about a king who must decide who is telling the truth and who is a lying.

A Puzzle for the King

Once upon a time, there lived a wise king who loved all the people in his vast kingdom. One day he decided to give away a large portion of his best land. He sent out messengers to the far corners of the kingdom.

"Write your name on a piece of paper and give it to us," the messengers shouted to everyone they met. "The king himself will draw a name, and the winner will be given a large piece of the finest land in the kingdom," they said.

After the messengers returned to the palace, they placed all of the papers into a large wooden barrel. The king stood on his royal balcony and drew a name.

"Hear ye, hear ye," he announced. "John Partridgebeak Baker is the winner of my choicest land."

Again the messengers were sent to the far corners of the kingdom. "John Partridgebeak Baker," they shouted, "the King invites you to come to the palace tomorrow at two o'clock to claim your prize."

The next day, at the exact moment that the town crier announced "Two o'clock and all is well," two men appeared at the palace door.

"I am John Partridgebeak Baker," cried the first man.

"I am John Partridgebeak Baker," echoed the second.

Which man was the true John Partridgebeak Baker? How could the wise king know which man should receive the prize?

Talk About the Story

Discuss possible endings for the story. One answer is at the end of this session.

Scripture

Today Jesus tells us how to recognize a genuine Christian. Read John 13:31–35.

> A reading from the holy gospel according to John
>
> After Judas had gone, Jesus said: "My children, I will be with you for a little while longer. Then you will look for me, but you won't find me. I tell you just as I told the people, 'You cannot go where I am going.'

"But I am giving you a new command. You must love each other, just as I have loved you. If you love each other, everyone will know that you are my disciples."

The gospel of the Lord.

Reflection

What did you hear Jesus say? Do you know anyone who seems to match Jesus' description of a true disciple?

Journal

See page 22 of your journal.

Prayer

Place a pretty container of blessed water on the prayer table along with a Bible. Then pray:
Jesus, our great friend,
you said, "Love one another
as I have loved you."
Place within our hearts
your spirit of love. Amen.

Blessing

Bless each other's hearts with the water, saying:

(Name),
you are a true disciple of Jesus.
May you be blessed, in the name of the Father, and of the Son, and of the Holy Spirit. Amen.

Possible Answer to the King's Puzzle

The king could ask each man to write his name on a piece of paper. Then he could compare the handwriting to the original signature.

Sixth Sunday of Easter

Jesus Makes Promises

Based on John 14:23 – 26

Opening Question

What are some things you like about your church?

Journal

See page 23, part 1 of your journal.

Story

Read the following story and see what Andy thought about his church.

Andy's Church

The fire trucks had arrived and the firefighters were drenching the small white church on the corner of Seventh and East Avenue. Andy looked with sadness at his faith community's gathering place. The insides were burnt and the beautiful stained-glass windows were all broken. Black, blistering smudges charred the once snow-white exterior.

"It was probably arson," a bystander said. "Eight churches have been burned this month."

"But why are they doing it?" another woman asked.

A television crew appeard on the scene. They took pictures of the smoldering church and the shocked bystanders. Seeing Andy, a reporter asked, "Now that your church is gone, what will you do?"

"Oh, "said Andy, "the church is not a building, the church is the people. God is always with us. We'll think of something."

Talk About the Story

Do you think Andy was right? What do you think he meant?

Scripture

In today's reading, Jesus makes promises to the church. Read John 14:23 – 26.

A reading from the holy gospel according to John

Jesus said: "If anyone loves me, they will obey me. Then my Father will love them, and we will come to them and live in them. But anyone who doesn't love me, won't obey me. What they have heard me say doesn't really come from me, but from the Father who sent me. I have told you these things while I am still with you. But the Holy Spirit will come and help you, because the Father will send the Spirit to take my place. The Spirit will teach you everything and will remind you of what I said while I was with you."

The gospel of the Lord.

Reflection

Imagine that you are with Andy during the television interview. What would you tell the reporter about Jesus' promises to the church?

Journal

See page 23, part 2 of your journal.

Prayer

Place a pretty bottle of oil or holy water on the prayer table along with your journals. Share journal prayers if you wish. Otherwise, say the following:

Ever-living God,
bless the people of your church.
Help us all to believe in the promises you have made.
We ask this through Jesus and the Holy Spirit,
who dwell within us forever and ever. Amen.

Blessing

Bless each other on the forehead or heart, and say:

(Name), you are blessed,
for you are God's dwelling place.
In the name of the Father, and of the Son, and of the Holy Spirit. Amen.

Seventh Sunday of Easter

We Are One with Jesus

Based on John 17:20–21

Story

Here is a story about a boy who showed what it means to be "at one" with someone.

The Boy of Peace

Michael and Mandy are twins. Their Mom says that they were born fighting. They haven't stopped in nine years.

One day, Michael and Mandy asked their parents if they could invite their friend Cory to go with the family for their day at the state park. Mom and Dad agreed, but they warned the twins yet again about their fighting.

When the day came, Michael and Mandy rushed to the car. Mom and Dad watched in distress as the two started to argue.

"You have to sit in the middle. I sat in the middle the last time, when Uncle Jim was with us."

"I can't sit in the middle. I have to sit by a window or I'll get sick. If I get sick, I'll be sure to get sick all over you!"

"Well, I can't sit in the middle. My legs are longer than yours. I'll be too uncomfortable. Besides, it's my turn."

"No it isn't! I sat in the middle two times before."

"Did not!"

"Did too!"

"Mom!"

"Dad!"

Mom and Dad both took a deep breath. But before they could say anything, Cory said, "If it's okay, I'd like to sit in the middle. That way I can sit next to both my best friends."

Everyone turned toward Cory, and for a moment, no one spoke. Then Mom said with a smile, "Of course, Cory." And everyone piled into the car.

After several miles of peaceful riding, Cory said to the twins, "You two sure are lucky to have each other. I keep asking my parents for a brother or sister, but they always say, 'We'll see.' I know that means no. But you'll always have a friend, no matter what."

After a few moments, Michael said, "Yeah. Mandy's a pain sometimes, but I'm glad she's my sister and my twin."

Mandy said, "I feel the same way about you."

Michael reached across Cory and gave his sister a friendly nudge. Cory put his arms around his two friends and sighed a happy sigh.

"Cory," Dad said, "you can come with us any time."

Talk About the Story

If you were in the back seat with Michael and Mandy, what might you have done? What helps you get along with your friends?

Scripture

At the last supper, Jesus gave his disciples a message about being "at one." Read John 17:20–21.

> A reading from the holy gospel according to John
>
> Jesus prayed to God: "Father, I am not praying just for these followers. I am also praying for everyone else who will have faith because of what my followers will say about me. I want all of them to be one with each other, just as I am one with you and you are one with me. I also want them to be one with us. Then the people of this world will believe that you sent me."
>
> The gospel of the Lord.

Reflection

Imagine you are one of the disciples. What did you hear Jesus say?

Journal

See page 24 of your journal.

Prayer

Prepare the prayer table with a container of oil or blessed water and a Bible. Then pray:

God of peace and unity,
we are at one
with you and your Son, Jesus.
Help us to be at one with others
so the world may be at peace.
We ask this in the name of Jesus,
the Prince of Peace. Amen.

Blessing

Bless each other with oil or water, saying:

(Name), you are a messenger of peace.
In the name of the Father,
and of the Son,
and of the Holy Spirit. Amen.

Pentecost

The Breath of God

Based on John 20:19–23

Opening Activities

Choose one or both of the following:

1. Have you ever "had the wind knocked out of you"? Or have you ever seen anyone give CPR (cardio-pulmonary resuscitation) to someone who was not breathing? Tell about it.

2. Put your hand in front of your nose or mouth, and see if you can feel your breath. Move your hand away from your face little by little until you can't feel your breath.

Story

Here is a story about how someone's breath saved a life.

The Breath of Life

"Oh, Mom, do I have to?" whined Cassie.

"Yes, I'll only be gone for an hour," her mother promised. "I need to do some errands."

Cassie did not want to babysit her two-year-old sister, Beth, but she had no choice. She decided to read her library book to help pass the time. Cassie left Beth in her highchair while she ran to her bedroom to get the book.

As she was rummaging through her room, she heard a loud thud come from the kitchen. Then all was quiet. Cassie ran into the kitchen and found Beth lying on the floor.

"Beth!" she screamed and stared at the baby. Cassie saw that Beth's eyes were closed and she was not breathing!

"Help me, oh, God, help me!" she prayed like she never prayed before. Just at that moment, through the kitchen window, Cassie saw her neighbor, Mrs. Barker, turn into the driveway. "A nurse, Mrs. Barker is a nurse," she said to herself. Cassie yelled through the screen door for help.

Within seconds Mrs. Barker was in the kitchen. "Cassie, call 911," Mrs. Barker said as she knelt next to Beth. While Cassie was on the phone, she could see Mrs. Barker place her mouth over Beth's mouth and breathe into her.

Soon Beth was gasping for air. A little pink glow was returning to her cheeks. Mrs. Barker smiled and stroked the little girl's forehead until the paramedics arrived.

"She's going to be all right," Cassie heard someone say.

"Oh, dear God, thank you. Thank you for the breath of life."

Talk About the Story

If you were Cassie, how would you have felt that day? If you were Mrs. Barker or Cassie's mom, what would your feelings have been?

Journal

See page 25, part 1 of your journal.

Scripture

Cassie thanked God for the breath of life for Beth. Read John 20:19–23 to see how Jesus gives the breath of life.

> **A reading from the holy gospel according to John**
>
> The disciples were afraid of the Jewish leaders, and on the evening of that same Sunday they locked themselves in a room. Suddenly, Jesus appeared in the middle of the group. He greeted them and showed them his hands and his side. When the disciples saw the Lord, they became very happy.
>
> After Jesus had greeted them again, he said, "I am sending you, just as the Father has sent me." Then he breathed on them and said, "Receive the Holy Spirit. If you forgive anyone's sins, they will be forgiven. But if you don't forgive their sins, they will not be forgiven."
>
> **The gospel of the Lord.**

Reflection

Imagine you were with the disciples that Pentecost evening. What would you tell your family about Jesus' visit?

Journal

See page 25, part 2 of your journal.

Prayer

Light a candle, and then place a jar or tin can over the flame until the fire dies out. Explain to your child that fire needs oxygen. We are like candles. We need the breath of God (oxygen) so that we can burn brightly with the love of the Holy Spirit (flame).

Relight the candle and place it on the prayer table along with the Bible, and pray:

Come, God, giver of gifts,
breathe into us the gift
of the Holy Spirit.
Come, Holy Spirit,
fill the hearts of your faithful,
and kindle in us the fire of your love.
Alleluia.

Blessing

Pass the lighted candle from person to person while saying:

(Name), you are blessed.
The fire of God's love is always with you.

Ordinary Time

It's not Lent or Easter. It's not Advent or Christmas. It's Ordinary Time. But that doesn't mean it's not important. It's like the everyday life that we all live. We get up. We go to school or to work. We prepare and eat meals and clean up. We say good morning and good night to those we love. We talk about our day and learn new things about ourselves and each other. It doesn't seem too special. But because we do these things, the bond of love between family and friends grows stronger and deeper. When special times do come — good and bad — we can celebrate or cry together because we are bound together by love.

During Ordinary Time in the church, we focus on the teachings of Jesus that show us how to live as his disciples every day, not just on Sundays and holidays. We do the ordinary things that Christians do: pray and try to live as Jesus would want us to. That's not always easy, but Jesus is always teaching us how.

Ordinary Time is the name given to two periods during the year: the short time between Christmas and Lent, and the long time between Pentecost and Advent. Most Sundays during this time don't have real names, just numbers. That's really why it's called "ordinary." It's the time that is ordered, or counted, rather than named. These days may be ordinary, but they sure count for a lot!

Trinity Sunday

The Mystery of God

Based on John 16:12–15

Opening Question

How can you know someone you have never seen?

> Try this. See how much you can find out about the person who wrote this letter.

> Dear Jay,
> Happy Birthday! What a joy to have a son like you! I hope you are enjoying your visit with Grandma. Your father is on his annual fishing trip, but he will be back in time for your birthday party on Sunday.
>
> I had to close the travel agency at noon today because the computer broke down. I enjoyed my unexpected afternoon off. Mary came over. She promised to help decorate your birthday cake. What a good friend! See you Sunday.
>
> I love you,
> Mom

Talk About the Letter

What did you find out about the person who wrote this letter?

Scripture

Just as this letter tells you something about Jay's mom, so scripture helps us understand a little about the mystery of God that we call the Trinity. Read John 16:12–15.

> A reading from the holy gospel according to John
>
> Jesus said to his disciples: "I have much more to say to you, but right now it would be more than you could understand. The Spirit shows what is true and will come and guide you into the full truth. The Spirit does not speak on his own. He will tell you only what he has heard from me, and he will let you know what is going to happen. The Spirit will bring glory to me by taking my message and telling it to you. Everything that the Father has is mine. That is why I have said that the Spirit takes my message and tells it to you."
>
> The gospel of the Lord.

Reflection

This passage is hard to understand. What did you hear about God, Jesus and the Holy Spirit? Did you get any new clues to the mystery of God? What questions would you ask Jesus? (Parent, you may need to read each sentence slowly and then talk about it.)

Journal

See page 26 of your journal.

Prayer

Place a bowl of water and three candles of the same size on the prayer table. Light the candles. With the assistance of your child, tip the candles so that the three individual flames make one large flame. (Protect the tablecloth with paper.) Then say:

There is one God with three divine persons.

Remove one candle and hold it up, saying:

Gift-giver, Creator, Loving Parent, God above all gods.
Add names from your journal.

Lift up the second candle, saying:

Jesus, Prince of Peace, Savior, Son of God.
Add names from your journal.

Lift up the third candle, saying:

Holy Spirit, Helper, Giver of Courage and Unity.
Add names from your journal.

We believe in you, Father, Son and Holy Spirit. Amen.

Blessing

Each person dips a hand into the water and makes the sign of the cross:

In the name of the Father, and of the Son, and of the Holy Spirit. Amen.

Body and Blood of Christ

A Precious Gift

Based on Luke 9:11–17

Opening Question

Did you ever give something away and unexpectedly get something better in return? What do you have that is precious and would be difficult to give away?

Journal

See page 27, part 1 of your journal.

Story

Imagine that you are living two thousand years ago. Life was very different then. This story is about a boy who struggled with a decision to share something precious.

Micah's Bread

"Mm-mmm," Micah murmured as he awoke. The smell of freshly baked bread filled his small room. The rattling cart that had awakened him was far down the street. Now the only sound was the clump clump of Aunt Chloe's crutch on the cold clay floor. Micah sleepily opened the drapery that separated his room from the rest of the small house. He could see his aunt take the goatskin of milk and pour it into the pitcher.

"Hurry, Micah," Aunt Chloe commanded. "You must go to the market alone today. My foot is still too sore to walk."

Micah shivered with excitement. "I'm going to the market alone today. I'm going to sell the loaves all by myself." He pictured himself returning with the money and the empty baskets. His aunt would smile and say, "What a fine young man you are becoming."

Aunt Chloe interrupted his thoughts. "Micah, hurry, the bread is ready." He dressed quickly. His aunt helped him put the two large baskets on Abdul's back, and Micah and the little donkey started off.

Micah and Abdul passed the pasture where Seth the shepherd was herding his sheep. On the mountainside, a man was talking to a large crowd of people. Micah had never seen so many people in Bethsaida before. "That's strange," he thought, but hurried on so he could get the best place at the market.

There was no need to hurry. The marketplace was almost deserted. Where could everyone be?

Micah tied Abdul to a palm tree and put the baskets on the ground. He sat in the sun and brushed off the hungry flies that buzzed around the bread.

Sales were slow. An hour passed slowly. Micah was beginning to feel bored when a vendor yelled, "Trade me two of your loaves for two fish." Micah had so many loaves left, he thought Aunt Chloe would not mind. Another hour passed. He sold three more loaves, but there were still five left. Micah was tired and discouraged. The day was not turning out the way he had pictured it. "I'd better start back, or Aunt Chloe will scold me for being late," he thought.

Micah packed the baskets on the donkey's back. "Abdul, let's go."

They passed Seth with his sheep. He was carrying a little lamb on his shoulder. "Father used to carry me on his shoulders, too. If Father and Mother were here, I would not have to worry about selling all the loaves," Micah said to Abdul.

Micah remembered his mother's laughter as she and his father danced around the table with Micah perched on his father's shoulders. They were a happy family then. But a great sickness had taken them. Micah was sent to live with Aunt Chloe, who complained about everything. Micah missed his parents very much.

As Micah walked along, he noticed the crowd of people again. Now they were sitting on the hillside. He could sell the five remaining loaves here. He shivered, this time nervously. "Loaves for sale," he cried as he bravely walked into the crowd.

"We have all walked a long way, and we are very hungry and tired," one man told him. "The Teacher is asking for bread and fish."

By this time the sun was low in the sky and casting long shadows on the grass. Aunt Chloe would be worried. Micah could give the Teacher the bread and tell Aunt Chloe he was robbed, but his father and mother had always told him to be honest. Aunt Chloe would be angry either way. The worst part is that she would not scold him. She would just say, "I knew you were too young to sell the loaves alone."

The Teacher looked so kind. Micah had heard rumors that he healed the blind and cured the sick. "I wish he would make Aunt Chloe happier," he thought.

A baby started crying. Micah looked up. The Teacher put the baby on his shoulders and walked over to Micah.

"Micah," he said, "would you share your bread with this crowd?" Seeing the child on his shoulder, Micah had the strangest, nicest feeling that his father and mother were right there.

"Micah, your Aunt Chloe will understand. There are so many hungry people."

Micah stood up and handed the basket to the Teacher. He felt dazed as he watched the Teacher bless the bread and then the fish. His disciples fed the entire crowd with Micah's bread and fish. After the people ate, the men filled twelve baskets with the leftovers. The Teacher walked over to Micah, smiling a broad smile. He handed Micah a basket overflowing with bread and fish. The bread was brown and glistening, and the fragrance was better than anything he had every smelled.

"Micah, take these to your Aunt Chloe, and wish her peace," he said. The Teacher carried the basket to the tree where Abdul was patiently waiting. Even Abdul looked surprised.

The sun was behind the grove of olive trees when Micah arrived at the small, whitewashed hut. Aunt Chloe had already put a candle in the window and was peering out the door.

"Aunt Chloe, he knew our names!" Micah exclaimed.

His aunt didn't even ask who. Her brown eyes became gentle and warm. "I know," she said softly, "What a fine young man you are. Let's break bread and eat."

Talk About the Story

If I were Micah, I would _____ .

Scripture

The story about Micah is similar to the one found in Luke 9:10 – 17. As you read the gospel, imagine that you are one of the people on the hillside listening to Jesus.

A reading from the holy gospel according to Luke

The apostles came back and told Jesus everything they had done. He then took them with him to the village of Bethsaida, where they could be alone. But a lot of people found out about this and followed him. Jesus welcomed them. He spoke to them about God's kingdom and healed everyone who was sick.

Late in the afternoon the twelve apostles came to Jesus and said, "Send the crowd to the villages and farms around here. They need to find a place to stay and something to eat. There is nothing in this place. It is like a desert!"

Jesus answered, "You give them something to eat."

But they replied, "We have only five small loaves of breads and two fish. If we are going to feed all these people, we will have to go and buy food." There were about five thousand men in the crowd.

Jesus said to his disciples, "Have the people sit in groups of fifty." They did this, and all the people sat down. Jesus took the five loaves and the two fish. He looked up toward heaven and blessed the food. Then he broke the bread and fish and handed them to his disciples to give to the people.

Everyone ate all they wanted. What was left over filled twelve baskets.

The gospel of the Lord.

Reflection

If you were in the crowd sitting on the hillside, what would you have observed?

Journal

See page 27, part 2 of your journal.

Optional Activity

Many cultures use bread as a basic food. With your child, discover the different types of bread that are availabe at your local bakery or grocery store (for example, pita, french, matzoh, tortilla, whole wheat, rye). If you like to bake your own bread, let your child assist. Then, before eating the bread, break it and thank God for the bread of life.

Prayer

Place some bread on the prayer table. Use a round loaf or some other special bread, if possible. Lift up the bread as an offering, and say:

Dear God,
you are the source of all that is good.
Thank you for the many gifts you give us.
Help us to share these gifts with others.
We ask this through Jesus, the Bread of Life. Amen.

Blessing

Break off a small piece of bread for yourself and pass the loaf on to the others. As each person breaks off a piece, extend your hands over that person, and pray:

(Name), taste and see the goodness of the Lord.

Body and Blood of Christ

Second Sunday in Ordinary Time

Jesus Is a Faithful Friend

Based on John 2:1 – 12

Opening Question

Can you think of a time when you were faithful to your word? Tell about it.

Journal

See page 28, part 1 of your journal. There you will find a puzzle. All the answers have something to do with keeping promises. The answers are on the next page.

Scripture

God made a covenant with the people many years before Jesus was born. God said, "I am your God, and you are my people." The gospel writers often used symbols to help us understand this covenant. Today's scripture reminds us that Jesus, like God, is a faithful friend. It is helpful to remember that the gospel writers saw Jesus as the bridegroom and the church as the bride.

> A reading from the holy gospel according to John
>
> Mary, the mother of Jesus, was at a wedding feast in the village of Cana in Galilee. Jesus and his disciples had also been invited and were there.
>
> When the wine was all gone, Mary said to Jesus, "They don't have any more wine."
>
> Jesus replied, "Mother, my time has not yet come! You must not tell me what to do."
>
> Mary then said to the servants, "Do whatever Jesus tells you to do."
>
> At the feast there were six stone water jars that were used by the people for washing themselves in the way that their religion said they must. Each jar held about twenty or thirty gallons. Jesus told the servants to fill them to the top with water. Then after the jars had been filled, he said, "Now take some water and give it to the man in charge of the feast."
>
> The servants did as Jesus told them, and the man in charge drank some of the water that had now turned into wine. He did not know where the wine had come from, but the servants did. He called the bridegroom over and said, "The best wine is always served first. Then after the guests have had plenty, the other wine is served. But you have kept the best until last!"
>
> This was Jesus' first miracle, and he did it in the village of Cana in Galilee. There Jesus showed his glory, and his disciples put their faith in him. After this, he went with his mother, his brothers, and his disciples to the town of Capernaum, where they stayed for a few days.
>
> The gospel of the Lord.

Reflection

If you were at the wedding in Cana, what would have surprised you?

Journal

See page 28, part 2 of your journal.

Prayer and Blessing

Fill glasses with grape juice and set them on the prayer table. Today's prayer models a variety of toasts about God, each other and faithfulness.

Lift up the glasses of juice and propose a toast such as:

Faithful God, we honor you and thank you for your friendship.
Response: **Yes. Amen!** *(Sip from the glass.)*

We celebrate your love and the love we have for each other.
Response: **Yes. Amen!** *(Sip from the glass.)*

Blessed be your name, now and forever.
Response: **Yes. Amen!** *(Sip from the glass.)*

Let us toast each other with a blessing.
(Make up your own, for example, [Name], **you are a gift of God to me.)**

Response after each: **Yes. Amen!** *(Sip from the glass.)*
(Name), **you are a reminder of God's faithfulness.**

Puzzle Answers

pact, loyal, vow, promise, allegiance, marriage, friendship, engagement ring.

Third Sunday in Ordinary Time

Jesus Sets Us Free

Based on Luke 4:14–21

Opening Questions

Have you ever been cooped up in a car or house for a long time? How did it feel when you finally got out?

Journal

See page 29, part 1 of your journal.

Story

There are many kinds of freedom. Read the following story and discover more about freedom.

Tyler's Field Trip

Tyler was excited. No way did he want to miss the bus, because today was the class field trip to the state historical museum. History was Tyler's favorite subject, and he couldn't wait to see the exhibits.

Luckily, the bus was right on time. It was filled with the usual assortment of people on their way to school or work or shopping. Tyler took his favorite seat in the middle of the bus, where he could see easily out the windows. When the bus passed a young woman jogging with her dog, Tyler suddenly realized that in his excitement that morning he had forgotten to feed his own dog. It was too late to go back home now. He'd miss the field trip.

Then Tyler remembered that the bus driver had an emergency phone. He had seen her use it before. Tyler approached the driver and asked, "Could you call my Mom and tell her to feed Goldie? I forgot to do it this morning."

"Young man," the driver growled, "I have a bus full of people to worry about. I'm not your personal secretary. Please take your seat."

As Tyler returned to his seat, he noticed a blind man slowly making his way to the rear exit by moving his cane back and forth in the aisle between the seats. The man almost tripped over a young woman's backpack. Tyler closed his eyes and tried to imagine what it would be like to ride the bus without being able to see. It was a strange feeling. How would he ever know when to get off?

Tyler was surprised when he opened his eyes and realized that his stop was next. The growly bus driver didn't even answer when Tyler said good-bye as he left the bus. The door slammed shut behind him. Tyler noticed that his classmates were already boarding the chartered bus for the field trip.

"Wait for me!" he yelled. Sprinting to the bus, he was glad to find that his best friend, Shane, had saved him a seat.

The trip and the museum took all morning. Tyler loved seeing all the old tools and pictures and hearing stories about the hardships the early settlers endured. After the tour, the class stopped at a nearby park for a picnic lunch. Tyler was pleasantly surprised when he saw his mother among the parents who had come to help.

Tyler's twin sister, Mary, was there too. Mary was in a special education class. She spotted Tyler, ran over and gave him a big hug in front of all his classmates. That was okay, though, because most of the kids in his class knew about Mary's special needs. She had started kindergarten with the rest of Tyler's class but had had difficulty keeping up. Mary was smart enough to know that she couldn't learn as quickly as her brother. Sometimes that made her very sad. Today, Mary's job was to help hand out the soda. She took her responsibility very seriously. Tyler was glad when even the class bully thanked Mary for his can of soda.

After lunch, everyone played softball. Someone yelled "Stupid!" when Tyler's friend Shane struck out. Shane's eyes filled with tears behind his glasses. Tyler shouted, "Hey, Shane, good try. We can practice some more tonight."

Next up to bat was Ann. She was a good, strong hitter who hardly ever struck out. But she couldn't run the bases. Her wheelchair made that difficult. She always asked Amy, the fastest runner in the class, to "be her legs." Amy made it to second base on the first pitch.

By two o'clock, the bus was headed back to school. Tyler was lucky. He got to ride home in the car with his Mom and Mary. As he relaxed in the car, he thought of all the people he had seen that day: the crabby bus driver, the blind passenger, his friend Shane, Ann in her wheelchair and his own sister, Mary. Each of them was limited in some way. Tyler wondered what he would do if he were in each of their situations. Then he turned to his sister, gave her a nudge and screwed up his face in the way he knew always made her laugh.

Talk About the Story

How would you have felt if you were one of the people in the story? What kind of help would you want?

Scripture

Almost everyone in the story "Tyler's Field Trip" was held captive in some way. Read Luke 4:14–21 and see what Jesus said about himself and captives.

> A reading from the holy gospel according to Luke
>
> Jesus returned to Galilee with the power of the Spirit. News about him spread everywhere. He taught in the Jewish meeting places, and everyone praised him.
>
> Jesus went back to Nazareth, where he had been brought up, and as usual he went to the meeting place on the Sabbath. When he stood up to read from the Scriptures, he was given the book of Isaiah the prophet. He opened it and read,
>
> "The Lord's Spirit has come to me, because he has chosen me to tell the good news to the poor. The Lord has sent me to announce freedom for prisoners, to give sight to the blind, to free everyone who suffers, and to say, 'This is the year the Lord has chosen.' "
>
> Jesus closed the book, then handed it back to the man in charge and sat down.
>
> Everyone in the meeting place looked straight at Jesus. Then Jesus said to them, "What you have just heard me read has come true today."
>
> The gospel of the Lord.

Reflection

Imagine that you were at the synagogue when Jesus read the scripture. What did you see? What did you hear about freedom?

Journal

See page 29, part 2 of your journal.

Prayer

Tie a helium-filled balloon to the prayer table. Have a marker nearby. Use your own words or the following prayer.

Jesus,
set us free
from our worries and troubles.
You are a model of compassion.
Help us to set others free
by being kind and thoughtful.
Amen.

Using the marker, print on the balloon a word that expresses a worry or concern. Release the balloon outside as you say the following or something similar:

Jesus, set us free. We trust in your care.

Fourth Sunday in Ordinary Time

Jesus, Model of Courage

Based on Luke 4:20–24, 28–30

Opening Question

Have you ever stood up for someone who needed help even though it was difficult for you? Tell about it.

Activity

Play the game "Stand Up," on page 155 in the supplement section of this book.

Scripture

Jesus stood up for what he believed even when people did not accept him. This story is a continuation of last week's gospel. Read Luke 4:20–24, 28–30.

> A reading from the holy gospel according to Luke

> Everyone in the Jewish meeting place looked straight at Jesus.
>   Then Jesus said to them, "What you have just heard me read has come true today."
>   All the people started talking about Jesus and were amazed at the wonderful things he said. They kept asking, "Isn't he Joseph's son?"
>   Jesus answered: "You certainly want to tell me this saying, 'Doctor, first make yourself well.' You will tell me to do the same things here in my own hometown that you heard I did in Capernaum. But you can be sure that no prophets are liked by the people of their own hometown."
>   When the people in the meeting place heard Jesus say this, they became so angry that they got up and threw him out of town. They dragged him to the edge of the cliff on which the town was built, because they wanted to throw him down from there. But Jesus slipped through the crowd and got away.

> The gospel of the Lord.

Reflection

If you had been in the crowd that day, what would you have said or done?

Journal

See page 30 of your journal.

Prayer

Place a Bible, a small bowl of bath oil, baby oil or vegetable oil, and the "Stand Up" cards on the prayer table. Lift the cards up in offering and pray the following, or use your own words.

Jesus, model of courage, strengthen us to stand up for what we believe.

Blessing

Bless the oil by making a sign of the cross over it while saying:

Creator of courage,
may this oil, which you have given us,
become a symbol of spiritual strength.

Take turns blessing each other on the forehead with the oil while saying:

May God bless you with courage.
In the name of the Father, and of the Son,
and of the Holy Spirit. Amen.

Fifth Sunday in Ordinary Time

Jesus Chooses His Disciples

Based on Luke 5:1 – 11

Opening Question

Have you ever been chosen to do something special in school, at home or at work? Talk about what happened.

Journal

See page 31, part 1 of your journal.

Scripture

When Jesus began his teaching, he looked for helpers who would make good leaders. Read Luke 5:1 – 11 to see how Jesus began choosing his apostles.

> A reading from the holy gospel according to Luke
>
> Jesus was standing on the shore of Lake Gennesaret, teaching the people as they crowded around him to hear God's message. Near the shore he saw two boats left there by some fishermen who had gone to wash their nets. Jesus got into the boat that belonged to Simon and asked him to row it out a little way from the shore. Then Jesus sat down in the boat to teach the crowd.
>
> When Jesus had finished speaking, he told Simon, "Row the boat out into the deep water and let your nets down to catch some fish."
>
> "Master," Simon answered, "we have worked hard all night long and have not caught a thing. But if you tell me to, I will let the nets down."
>
> They did it and caught so many fish that their nets began ripping apart. Then they signaled for their partners in the other boat to come and help them. The men came, and together they filled the two boats so full that they both began to sink.
>
> When Simon Peter saw this happen, he kneeled down in front of Jesus and said, "Lord, don't come near me! I am a sinner."
>
> Peter and everyone with him were completely surprised at all the fish they had caught. His partners James and John, the sons of Zebedee, were surprised too.
>
> Jesus told Simon, "Don't be afraid! From now on you will bring in people instead of fish." The men pulled their boats up on the shore. Then they left everything and went with Jesus.
>
> The gospel of the Lord.

Reflection

Imagine that you are in the boat and Jesus is talking with you. What does Jesus say? What do you say to Jesus? What is it like to be chosen by Jesus?

Journal

See page 31, part 2 of your journal.

Prayer

Parent: In advance, place a Bible and a pretty bottle of bath oil or vegetable oil on the prayer table. Begin with the following prayer, or use your own words.

Dear God,
thank you for choosing us to be your friends.
Help us to know what you want us to do.
We ask this favor in Jesus' name. Amen.

Blessing

Parent: Invite your child to hold the container of oil while you bless it with a sign of the cross while saying:

O Giver of Knowledge, bless this oil,
a symbol of spiritual strength.

Take turns blessing each other on the forehead with the oil while saying:

(Name), may you have the knowledge and courage to be what God wants you to be.
In the name of the Father, and of the Son,
and of the Holy Spirit. Amen.

Sixth Sunday in Ordinary Time

Jesus Teaches Us How to Be Happy

Based on Luke 6:17, 20–23

Opening Question

Have you ever experienced a mixed blessing? In other words, has an unfortunate event ever brought something good?

Journal

See page 32, part 1 of your journal.

Story

Here is a story about a family who experienced a blessing during a tragic time.

A Mixed Blessing

"Get up, Samantha. Wake up your brother, then pack clothes for at least a week."

Samantha sat on her bed, slightly dazed.

"What did you say, Mom?"

"Old Red is close to the fence in the backyard and we have to get out of the house. Quick, get your brother up and tell him."

Old Red was the family's pet name for the Red River, which flowed past their home. They loved the river. But every spring they were on a flood alert as the winter snow melted, causing Old Red to cross beyond its normal boundary.

Samantha raced into Brad's room and shook him until he woke up. "Get up! The river is overflowing its banks. Mom says to pack enough things for a week."

Brad, her older brother, jumped out of bed and dumped the contents of his top three dresser drawers into a large box on the floor. Mom had left it there yesterday with a command, "Clean this floor so I can at least change your sheets."

Brad's swiftness startled Samantha. She was anchored in the doorway gawking at him. He was a whirlwind.

"Hey, Sis, get going! We don't have much time," he said as he raced past her. "I'll see if Dad needs help."

Samantha got out her blue suitcase and carefully put in it a week's supply of clothes and a hand-carved wooden box that held some of her most cherished treasures, including the gold locket Aunt Bess gave her last Christmas. She was wondering how many books she should take along when her mother shouted, "Samantha, hurry, the water is almost to the driveway, and we have to leave *now.*"

As Samantha reached the open front door, she heard an unfamiliar sound. The low slapping she had been hearing almost unconsciously was now much louder. It was more like a hungry animal creeping slowly toward its prey. Fear grabbed her. Just then, Dad pulled the switch that turned off all the electricity. The complete blackness startled her, and a new wave of fear clutched her insides.

"Mom!" Her voice was higher than usual. "Where are you?"

"Here, Samantha, take my hand," she heard Dad say as they fumbled out the front door. "Everyone is in the car."

She could feel the cold grip of Old Red creeping up over her sneakers as she and Dad splashed through the slush in the yard. The river had turned into an enemy, threatening their security.

As they backed out of the driveway, the first wink of morning broke the blackened night. She could see someone's garbage can floating in their backyard. She wanted to say something about it but felt a blanket of sad silence folding around her family.

Ten minutes later, Samantha and her mother were bringing their suitcases into Grandma's home. Grandma live on a hill overlooking the swollen river.

Dad turned to Brad and said, "We have a historic town here, and we need to save it. Brad, I'm going down to help sandbag that levee. We still have a chance to prevent major damage to our own home. You've been bagging for the last three days. Do you want to stay at Grandma's?"

"No, I'm coming with to help save the town, Dad."

They left Samantha and her mother at the doorstep and hurried down the hill to join the weary volunteers.

Later, Samantha sipped hot cocoa while Grandma and her mother talked about the flood. "We are so blessed," Grandma said.

"Blessed!" Samantha thought, "When our home is ready to be eaten up by Old Red?"

"Blessed?" her mother questioned out loud.

"Yes, our town is blessed. Volunteers from all over Minnesota and the Dakotas have been sandbagging for four days and nights. The river should crest today and begin to recede. Oh, thanks be to God. Without those generous and courageous people our town would not be saved. We are blessed."

Talk About the Story

If you were Samantha, how would you have felt when Grandma said, "We're blessed"?
Can you think of another example of a time when you had mixed blessings?

Scripture

Last week we read about Jesus inviting apostles to follow him. In today's gospel, Jesus is preparing his disciples to be ready for mixed blessings.

A reading from the holy gospel according to Luke

Jesus and his apostles went down from the mountain and came to some flat, level ground. Many other disciples were there to meet him. Large crowds of people from all over Judea, Jerusalem, and the coastal cities of Tyre and Sidon were there too.

Jesus looked at his disciples and said: "God will bless you people who are poor. His kingdom belongs to you! God will bless you hungry people. You will have plenty to eat! God will bless you people who are crying. You will laugh!

"God will bless you when others hate you and won't have anything to do with you. God will bless you when people insult you and say cruel things about you, all because you are a follower of the Son of Man! Long ago your own people did these same things to the prophets.

"So when this happens to you, be happy and jump for joy! You will have a great reward in heaven."

The gospel of the Lord.

Reflection

Did Jesus say anything that surprised you? Is there anything that you did not understand? Talk it over with your family.

Journal

See page 32, part 2 of your journal.

Prayer

Parent: Blessed are the poor in spirit, because they share what they have.
Child: Happy are we who hope in God.

Parent: Blessed are those who hunger for God.
Child: Happy are we who hope in God.

Parent: Blessed are those who believe that God can change sadness to joy.
Child: Happy are we who hope in God.

Parent: Blessed are those who are peacemakers.
Child: Happy are we who hope in God.

Parent: God, we pray this prayer in Jesus' name for ever and ever. Amen.

Blessing

Give each other a hug, and say:

Blessed are you *(Name)*, for God is always with you.

Seventh Sunday in Ordinary Time

Becoming Like God

Based on Luke 6:27–37

Opening Question

In what ways are you and I alike? In what ways are we different?

Newspaper Story

Sometimes people are recognized by their resemblances to other family members. Read the following newspaper article.

Woman Recognized by Resemblance to Mother

Eagle Ridge, MO: Susan Blake of Los Angeles was found by a park ranger yesterday in a wooded area north of Eagle Ridge. Blake had apparently been struck by a falling tree branch while bird-watching. She was dazed and unable to remember her name, and no identification was found on her. Park ranger Bob Blue noticed a close resemblance to local mayor Marian Blake. Mayor Blake was called to the scene, and she identified the dazed woman as her daughter, Susan, of Los Angeles, who was visiting her.

"The injured woman looked just like our mayor, so I knew it must be her daughter," Ranger Blue reported. Ms. Blake was treated and released from Eagle Ridge Hospital today.

Talk About the Story

Susan Blake was recognized because she resembled her mother. Discuss how you and your child are alike aside from physical appearances (attitudes, habits, ways of doing things, similar expressions when talking, likes and dislikes).

Scripture

In today's gospel, Jesus invites us to resemble God by our actions and attitudes. Read Luke 6:27–37.

A reading from the holy gospel according to Luke

Jesus said to his disciples: "This is what I say to all who will listen to me: Love your enemies, and be good to everyone who hates you. Ask God to bless anyone who curses you, and pray for everyone who is cruel to you. If someone slaps you on one cheek, don't stop that person from slapping you on the other cheek. If someone wants to take your coat, don't try to keep back your shirt. Give to everyone who asks and don't ask people to return what they have taken from you. Treat others just as you want to be treated.

"If you love only someone who loves you, will God praise you for that? Even sinners love people who love them. If you are kind only to someone who is kind to you, will God be pleased with you for that? Even sinners are kind to people who are kind to them. If you lend money only to someone you think will pay you back, will God be pleased with you for that? Even sinners lend to sinners because they think they will get it all back.

"But love your enemies and be good to them.

"Lend without expecting to be paid back. Then you will get a great reward, and you will be the true children of God in heaven. He is good even to people who are unthankful and cruel. Have pity on others, just as your Father has pity on you.

"Don't judge others, and God will not judge you. Don't be hard on others, and God will not be hard on you. Forgive others, and God will forgive you."

The gospel of the Lord.

Reflection

Imagine that you are one of the disciples. What do you hear Jesus asking you to do so you can be more like God?

Journal

See page 33 of your journal.

Prayer and Blessing

Make a small cross on your forehead, saying:
God, Giver of wisdom, bless us that we may have thoughts like Jesus.

Make a small cross on your lips, saying:
God, giver of the word, help us to speak with kindness and respect.

Make a small cross over your heart, saying:
God, source of love, open our hearts to love you and others.

Make a cross on each hand, saying:
Gentle God, bless our hands that we may help and never hurt another.
We ask this in Jesus' name. Amen.

Eighth Sunday in Ordinary Time

Being Trustworthy

Based on Luke 6:39–45

Opening Questions

Sometimes people don't say what they really mean, and at first we are puzzled. Here is a situation.

Some of your classmates decide to meet in the park at four o'clock to go to the movies. You arrive five minutes early, and no one is there. You wait and wait, but no one comes. Later you discover that they all met at three o'clock. The next time they promise to meet at a certain time, how might you feel? How might you handle it?

Here is another situation. You were told not to swim in the river because of the strong currents. A friend about your size tells you that she or he just received an intermediate swimming certificate and knows how to save you in case the currents are too strong. What would be some questions you would ask yourself?

Journal

See page 34, part 1 of your journal.

Scripture

Jesus tells his disciples to be trustworthy and to "practice what they preach." In Luke 6:39–45, read the many examples that Jesus gives.

> A reading from the holy gospel according to Luke
>
> Jesus used some sayings as he spoke to the people. He said: "Can one blind person lead another blind person? Won't they both fall into a ditch?
>
> "Are students better than their teacher? But when they are fully trained, they will be like their teacher.
>
> "You can see the speck in your friend's eye. But you don't notice the log in your own eye. How can you say, 'My friend, let me take the speck out of your eye,' when you don't see the log in your own eye? You showoffs! First, get the log out of your own eye. Then you can see how to take the speck out of your friend's eye.
>
> "A good tree cannot produce bad fruit, and a bad tree cannot produce good fruit. You can tell what a tree is like by the fruit it produces. You cannot pick figs or grapes from thorn bushes. Good people do good things because of the good in their hearts. Bad people do bad things because of the evil in their hearts. Your words show what is in your hearts."
>
> The gospel of the Lord.

Reflection

If you were in the crowd and someone asked you "What did Jesus say?" what would you have told them? (Parent, if your child is stuck, discuss the meaning of the images mentioned in the reading.)

Journal

See page 34, part 2 of your journal.

Prayer

God, we can always trust you.
Help us to be trustworthy
so that our actions may match our words.
We ask this in Jesus' name. Amen.

Blessing

Make a small sign of the cross on your lips and over your heart while praying:

God bless our words *(bless lips)*
that they may match what is in our hearts *(bless heart).*

Ninth Sunday in Ordinary Time

God Has a Big Heart

Based on Luke 7:1 – 10

Opening Activity

Talk about God's creative masterpieces found in nature. For example:

- Look at the tiny shapes in snowflakes. Each one is different.
- Look at the beautiful colors in flowers. Do you have a favorite flower? a favorite color?
- When looking at the ocean or sky, we know that God is awesome.
- God must be very beautiful to make such a lovely sunset.
- Look at God's stars in the vast universe. How generous God is to give us lights at night and one big glow of sun in the daytime. God must have a big heart to give us so much.

Continue thanking and praising God as you and your child look for various gifts of God.

Journal

See page 35 of your journal.

Scripture

In Luke 7:1 – 10 you will read about a man who knew that Jesus had a big heart.

A reading from the holy gospel according to Luke

After Jesus had finished teaching the people, he went to Capernaum. In that town an army officer's servant was sick and about to die. The officer liked this servant very much. And when he heard about Jesus, he sent some Jewish leaders to ask him to come and heal the servant.

The leaders went to Jesus and begged him to do something. They said, "This man deserves your help! He loves our nation and even built us a meeting place." So Jesus went with them.

When Jesus was not far from the house, the officer sent some friends to tell him, "Lord, don't go to any trouble for me! I am not good enough for you to come into my house. And I am certainly not worthy to come to you. Just say the word, and my servant will get well. I have officers who give orders for me, and I have soldiers who take orders from me. I can say to one of them, 'Go!' and he goes. I can say to another, 'Come!' and he comes. I can say to my servant, 'Do this!' and he will do it."

When Jesus heard this, he was so surprised that he turned and said to the crowd following him, "In all of Israel I've never found anyone with this much faith!"

The officer's friends returned and found the servant well.

The gospel of the Lord.

Reflection

What would it have been like to be the officer or the sick servant that day? What are some amazing things that God has done for you?

Prayer

Place the litanies you just wrote in the journals on the prayer table. Then begin praying:

God, generous gift-giver,
you have a big heart,
and you share so many gifts with us.
We thank and praise you for:

(Slowly read the litanies and responses from the journals.)

Conclude with:

We praise and thank you in the name of Jesus. Amen.

Blessing

Share some sign of affection with each other while saying:

You are God's generous gift to me.
I bless you in the name of the Father,
and of the Son, and of the Holy Spirit. Amen.

Tenth Sunday in Ordinary Time

God Lives Among Us

Based on Luke 7:11–17

Opening Question

This is the season when nature comes alive. What signs of renewed life have you observed recently?

Puzzle

Here is a puzzle for you to solve: If someone who died became alive again, like the trees and flowers do each spring, it would be a sign that _____ .
(Parent: Have your child turn to page 36, part 1 in the journal, or put the following on a separate piece of paper.)

___ ___ ____ __

___ _____ .

Ask your child to guess the missing letters, beginning with consonants, while you put the letters in the correct spaces. See the correct answer at the end of this session. (Also see page 36, part 1 of the adult journal.)

Scripture

In today's gospel, Luke 7:11–17, you will hear a story about a woman who knew for sure that God visited her.

> A reading from the holy gospel according to Luke
>
> Jesus and his disciples were on their way to the town of Nain, and a big crowd was going along with them. As they came near the gate of the town, they saw people carrying out the body of a widow's only son. Many people from the town were walking along with her.
>   When the Lord saw the woman, he felt sorry for her and said, "Don't cry!"
>   Jesus went over and touched the stretcher on which the people were carrying the dead boy. They stopped, and Jesus said, "Young man, get up!" The man sat up and began to speak. Jesus then gave him back to his mother.
>   Everyone was frightened and praised God. They said, "A great prophet is here with us! God has come to his people."
>   News about Jesus spread all over Judea and everywhere else in that part of the country.
>
> The gospel of the Lord.

Reflection

Pick a character in the scripture story you just read. What would it have been like to be that person?

Journal

See page 36, part 2 of your journal.

Prayer

Find something that represents "new life" and place it on the prayer table (for example, flowers, leaves, a picture of a baby, a picture of someone who died and is now experiencing new life in heaven, etc.). Then pray:

God, giver of life,
we thank you for your presence among us.
Thank you for your breath of life
in all living things.
Help us to respect that life.
We ask this in the name of Jesus. Amen.

Blessing

Place a bowl of water and a small branch for sprinkling on the prayer table. Bless each other with the water, saying:

(Name), I bless you in the name of God,
who gives you life.

Use the rest of the water to bless plants, flowers, trees or a garden.

Answer to Puzzle

God has come to the people.

Eleventh Sunday in Ordinary Time

Jesus Sees Our Hearts

Based on Luke 7:36–50

Opening Questions

Do you have any friends whom you did not like at first? What are some things you like about them now?

Journal

See page 37, part 1 of your journal.

Story

Here is a story about a teacher who saw good in all her students.

Sally's Gift

It was Mrs. Worthington's birthday, and the class had planned a surprise party for her. One of the parents decorated a special cake, and there was plenty of punch and cookies, too. Even the principal stopped by to wish her well. Now everyone "oohed" and "ahhed" as she unwrapped her presents.

Suddenly the class became silent as Mrs. Worthington picked up the last present. It was wrapped with wrinkled paper and had a few grease spots on it. Everyone knew it was from Sally. The teacher opened it carefully. She held up an old, worn teddy bear. No one "ooh-ed" or "ahh-ed" this time.

Mrs. Worthington smiled with delight. Hugging the bear she said, "I like this gift very much. I can tell this bear has been cherished and given lots of love. I'll keep it right by my books so I can see it every day."

Talk About the Story

Finish these sentences:

If I were the teacher, I would _____ .

If I were Sally, I would _____ .

If I were one of the students, I would _____ .

Scripture

Jesus finds goodness in everybody. Read Luke 7:36–50 to see what happened when Jesus visited Simon's house.

A reading from the holy gospel according to Luke

A Pharisee invited Jesus to have dinner with him. So Jesus went to the Pharisee's home and got ready to eat.

When a sinful woman in that town found out that Jesus was there, she bought an expensive bottle of perfume. Then she came and stood behind Jesus. She cried and started washing his feet with her tears and drying them with her hair. The woman kissed his feet and poured the perfume on them.

The Pharisee who had invited Jesus saw this and said to himself, "If this man really were a prophet, he would know what kind of woman is touching him! He would know that she is a sinner."

Jesus said to the Pharisee, "Simon, I have something to say to you."

"Teacher, what is it?" Simon replied.

Jesus told him, "Two people were in debt to a moneylender. One of them owed him five hundred silver coins, and the other owed him fifty. Since neither of them could pay him back, the moneylender said that they didn't have to pay him anything. Which one of them will like him most?"

Simon answered, "I suppose it would be the one who had owed more and didn't have to pay it back."

"You are right," Jesus said.

He turned toward the woman and said to Simon, "Have you noticed this woman? When I came into your home, you didn't give me any water so I could wash my feet. But she has washed my feet with her tears and dried them with her hair.

"You didn't greet me with a kiss, but from the time I came in, she has not stopped kissing my feet.

"You didn't even pour olive oil on my head, but she has poured expensive perfume on my feet.

"So I tell you that all her sins are forgiven, and that is why she has shown great love. But anyone who has been forgiven only a little will show only a little love."

Then Jesus said to the woman, "Your sins are forgiven."

Some other guests started saying to one another, "Who is this who dares to forgive sins?"

But Jesus told the woman, "Because of your faith, you are now saved. May God give you peace!"

The gospel of the Lord.

Reflection

If you had been invited to Simon's party, what would you have noticed? What qualities would Jesus have found in you?

Journal

See page 37, part 2 of your journal.

Prayer

Gather photos of people whom you would have invited to Simon's party. Or make a list of people you would have wanted Jesus to meet at the party. Place the photos or list on the prayer table. Then pray:

God,
you sent your Son, Jesus, for everyone.
Thank you for accepting and loving us all.
Help us to respect and accept others in Jesus' name.
Amen.

Blessing

Ask your child to lift up the guest list or photos, and pray:

God, you have surrounded us
with family and friends.
Bless us now
as we look for the good in each other.

Everyone makes the sign of the cross on themselves.

In the name of the Father,
and of the Son,
and of the Holy Spirit. Amen.

Twelfth Sunday in Ordinary Time

Getting to Know Jesus

Based on Luke 9:18 – 24

Opening Activity

Together, play "The Discovery Game" in the supplement, page 157.

Scripture

What are some ways you can discover more about your family and friends besides playing "The Discovery Game"?

Read Luke 9:18 – 24 and see what you can discover about Jesus.

A reading from the holy gospel according to Luke

When Jesus was alone praying, his disciples came to him, and he asked them, "What do people say about me?"

They answered, "Some say that you are John the Baptist or Elijah or a prophet from long ago who has come back to life."

Jesus then asked them, "But who do you say I am?"

Peter answered, "You are the Messiah sent from God."

Jesus strictly warned his disciples not to tell anyone what had happened.

Jesus told his disciples, "The nation's leaders, the chief priests, and the teachers of the Law of Moses will make the Son of Man suffer terribly. They will reject him and kill him, but three days later he will rise to life."

Then Jesus said to all the people: "If any of you want to be my followers, you must forget about yourself. You must take up your cross each day and follow me. If you want to save your life, you will destroy it. But if you give up your life for me, you will save it."

The gospel of the Lord.

Reflection

If Jesus were to ask you "Who do you say that I am?" what would you answer?

Journal

See page 38 of your journal.

Prayer

Place your journals on the prayer table. Take turns reading something you wrote about Jesus. After each statement, respond with "I believe in you, Jesus."

For example: Reader: **Jesus, you are the Son of God.**

Response: **I believe in you, Jesus.**

After the litany, conclude with:

God, thank you for giving us Jesus.
Help us to grow in faith.
We ask this in Jesus' name. Amen.

Blessing

Sign each other with a cross on the forehead, saying:

(Name), may you grow in friendship with Jesus.

Thirteenth Sunday in Ordinary Time

God's Call for Commitment

Based on Luke 9:57–62

Opening Question

Have you ever put all your energy into a project? Tell about it.

Activity

The following activities demand some dedication. Choose one of them, or design your own family summer project.

- Plan and assign tasks for a family vacation.
- Adopt a person who is confined to a home or a nursing care center because of age or illness. Each week, bring that person a flower or some other item from nature.
- As a family, help keep a section of your neighborhood or town clean of litter.
- Discuss some of your own commitments to the family. Encourage and thank the child for whatever he or she does on behalf of the family.

Journal

See page 39, part 1 of your journal.

Scripture

Jesus experienced how difficult total dedication can be. Read Luke 9:57–62 to see what Jesus has to say about commitment.

> A reading from the holy gospel according to Luke
>
> Along the way to Jerusalem someone said to Jesus, "I'll go anywhere with you!"
> Jesus said, "Foxes have dens, and birds have nests, but the Son of Man doesn't have a place to call his own."
> Jesus told someone else to come with him. But the man said, "Lord, let me wait until I bury my father."
> Jesus answered, "Let the dead take care of the dead, while you go and tell about God's kingdom."
> Then someone said to Jesus, "I want to go with you, Lord, but first let me go back and take care of things at home."
> Jesus answered, "Anyone who starts plowing and keeps looking back isn't worth a thing in God's kingdom!"
>
> The gospel of the Lord.

Reflection

You, too, are a follower of Jesus. What are some of the things you have to sacrifice in order to be a committed disciple?

Journal

See page 39, part 2 of your journal.

Prayer

Prepare a bowl of water and a branch for sprinkling. Invite each person to place his or her shoes or sandals on the prayer table as a symbol of following in Jesus' footsteps. Then begin with:

Jesus,
you walked from town to town
spreading the good news.
You are with us
on our life's journey.
Help us to be your dedicated disciples,
even when it is hard.

Blessing

Bless the shoes or sandals with holy water while saying:

God, bless these shoes. Let them remind us to walk in Jesus' footsteps.

Put on the shoes and then bless each other, saying:

(Name), may God give you strength
to be a dedicated disciple.
In the name of the Father,
and of the Son,
and of the Holy Spirit. Amen.

Fourteenth Sunday in Ordinary Time

Sharing the Excitement

Based on Luke 10:1 – 9

Opening Question

What are you enthusiastic or excited about this summer? Tell each other about it.

Story

A Gift of Enthusiasm

Elliot never did anything half-heartedly. When his mother asked him to take out the garbage, he jumped right up, grabbed the bag and zoomed out the door. When he waited for his turn to bat in a baseball game, he called out encouraging words to his teammates and jumped up and down when they made a hit; he was even encouraging when they struck out.

One day, Elliot and his friend Lois were playing in the park. After a while, they decided to rest on the steps of the bandstand. They chatted about school and family, and then Elliot started talking excitedly about the story of Jesus and his disciples that he had heard in church last Sunday. Lois was fascinated; she had never heard anyone talk about Jesus in this way before.

Mrs. Connolly from the parish happened to be sitting on a nearby bench. When the two children got up to continue playing, she called Elliot over to her.

"You have a great gift, Elliot. Your enthusiasm for telling the story of Jesus is a gift from God. You should consider spending your life sharing that gift."

And Elliot did.

In later years, when people asked him how he decided to spend his life telling people about Jesus, he said, "When I was ten years old, God gave me two gifts: an enthusiasm for spreading the good news of Jesus, and a wise lady who helped me see what a gift that is."

Journal

See page 40, part 1 of your journal.

Scripture

Read Luke 10:1 – 9 and see what Jesus told his disciples about evangelizing, which means "spreading the good news about God."

A reading from the holy gospel according to Luke

The Lord chose seventy-two other followers and sent them out two by two to every town and village where he was about to go.

He said to them: "A large crop is in the fields, but there are only a few workers. Ask the lord in charge of the harvest to send out workers to bring it in. Now go, but remember, I am sending you like lambs into a pack of wolves. Don't take along a moneybag or a traveling bag or sandals. And don't waste time greeting people on the road.

"As soon as you enter a home, say, 'God bless this home with peace.' If the people living there are peace-loving, your prayer for peace will bless them. But if they are not peace-loving, your prayer will return to you.

"Stay with the same family, eating and drinking whatever they give you, because workers are worth what they earn. Don't move round from house to house.

"If the people of a town welcome you, eat whatever they offer you. Heal their sick and say, 'God's kingdom will soon be here.' "

The gospel of the Lord.

Reflection

Imagine you are a disciple who will soon travel to neighboring towns to spread the good news. What advice that Jesus gave would you want to remember?

Journal

See page 40, part 2 of your journal.

Prayer and Blessing

O God, Great Teacher,
you know all things.
We thank you
for those who have helped us
learn about you.

Take turns mentioning names of those who have shared the good news about God with you.

Let us make a cross on our own foreheads.
God, bless our minds that we may know you.

Let us make a cross on our lips.
God, bless our lips that we may speak of you.

Let us make a cross over our hearts.
God, bless our hearts that we may love you.

Bless us as we spread your good news this week.

We ask this *(make the sign of the cross)*
in the name of the Father,
and of the Son,
and of the Holy Spirit. Amen.

Fifteenth Sunday in Ordinary Time
Being a Good Samaritan
Based on Luke 10:25–37

Opening Question

Was there ever a time when you found it hard to be kind to someone? Tell about it.

Activity

Play the "Who Are My Neighbors? Game" found in the supplement.

Scripture

In today's gospel, someone asks Jesus, "Who are my neighbors?" Read Luke 10:25–37, and see how Jesus answers.

> A reading from the holy gospel according to Luke

An expert in the Law of Moses stood up and asked Jesus a question to see what he would say. "Teacher," he asked. "What must I do to have eternal life?"

Jesus answered, "What is written in the Scriptures? How do you understand them?"

The man replied, "The Scriptures say, 'Love the Lord your God with all your heart, soul, strength, and mind.' They also say, 'Love your neighbors as much as you love yourself.' "

Jesus said, "You have given the right answer. If you do this, you will have eternal life."

But the man wanted to show that he knew what he was talking about. So he asked Jesus, "Who are my neighbors?"

Jesus replied: "As a man was going down from Jerusalem to Jericho, robbers attacked him and grabbed everything he had. They beat him up and ran off, leaving him half dead.

"A priest happened to be going down the same road. But when he saw the man, he walked by on the other side. Later a temple helper came to the same place. But when he saw the man who had been beaten up, he also went by on the other side.

"A man from Samaria then came traveling along that road. When he saw the man, he felt sorry for him and went over to him. He treated his wounds with olive oil and wine and bandaged them. Then he put him on his own donkey and took him to an inn, where he took care of him.

"The next morning he gave the innkeeper two silver coins and said, 'Please take care of the man. If you spend more than this on him, I will pay you when I return.' "

Then Jesus asked, "Which of these three people was a real neighbor to the man who was beaten up by robbers?"

The teacher answered, "The one who showed pity." Jesus said, "Go and do the same!"

The gospel of the Lord.

Reflection

How would you have felt if you were the injured man? the Samaritan?

Journal

See page 41 of your journal.

Prayer

Bring the "Who Are My Neighbors? Game" to the prayer table. Light a candle, and begin:

Jesus, Son of God,
you are our best example
for loving others.

You loved us so much
that you gave us your life.
Help us to be good neighbors
even when it is difficult.
We ask this in your name, Jesus.
Amen.

Blessing

Make a small sign of the cross on your child. Hug your child and say, "I love you."

Sixteenth Sunday in Ordinary Time

The Guest

Based on Luke 10:38 – 42

Opening Question

When you visit your grandparent(s), aunt, uncle or friend, what things do you enjoy? Is there anything that you wish were different?

Journal

See page 42, part 1 of your journal.

Scripture

Read Luke 10:38 – 42 to see what happened when Jesus visited two friends.

> **A reading from the holy gospel according to Luke**
>
> The Lord and his disciples were traveling along and came to a village. When they got there, a woman named Martha welcomed him into her home. She had a sister named Mary, who sat down in front of the Lord and was listening to what he said.
>
> Martha was worried about all that had to be done. Finally, she went to Jesus and said, "Lord, doesn't it bother you that my sister has left me to do all the work by myself? Tell her to come and help me!"
>
> The Lord answered, "Martha, Martha! You are worried and upset about so many things, but only one thing is necessary. Mary has chosen what is best, and it will not be taken away from her."
>
> **The gospel of the Lord.**

Reflection

What did you hear Jesus tell Martha and Mary? How would you feel if Jesus came to your home? What are some things that you would share with Jesus?

Journal

See page 42, part 2 of your journal.

Prayer

Spend some time sitting on a blanket at night looking at the stars, or walking in a place of natural beauty. Talk to your child of God's presence. Spend some time in quiet reflection too. On the way home, make a litany of praise recalling God's blessings (for example, "O God, you made the stars." Response: "Thank you, God, for being here").

Seventeenth Sunday in Ordinary Time

Ask and You Will Receive

Based on Luke 11:1–10

Opening Question

Talk about a time when you really needed help. What did you do? What happened?

Journal

See page 43, part 1 of your journal.

Story

Read "The Gift" on page 14. The story is about a girl who needed help.

Talk About the Story

If you were Judy, what might you have done? If you were Judy's parents, how would you have felt?

Scripture

In Luke 11:1–10, Jesus tells us what to do when we need help.

> A reading from the holy gospel according to Luke
>
> When Jesus had finished praying, one of his disciples said to him, "Lord, teach us to pray, just as John taught his followers to pray."
>
> So Jesus told them, "Pray in this way:
>
> 'Father, help us to honor your name. Come and set up your kingdom. Give us each day the food we need. Forgive our sins, as we forgive everyone who has done wrong to us. And keep us from being tempted.' "
>
> Then Jesus went on to say: "Suppose one of you goes to a friend in the middle of the night and says, 'Let me borrow three loaves of bread. A friend of mine has dropped in, and I don't have a thing for him to eat.' And suppose your friend answers, 'Don't bother me! The door is bolted, and my children and I are in bed. I cannot get up to give you something.'
>
> "He may not get up and give you the bread, just because you are his friend. But he will get up and give you as much as you need, only because you are not ashamed to keep on asking.
>
> "So I tell you to ask and you will receive, search and you will find, knock and the door will be opened for you. Everyone who asks will receive, everyone who searches will find, and the door will be opened for everyone who knocks."
>
> The gospel of the Lord.

Reflection

What do you think Jesus meant when he said, "Ask and you will receive, search and you will find, knock and the door will be opened for you"?

We know that God hears our prayers, but we might wonder why God doesn't always give us what we ask for. Do you have any ideas about this?

(Parent: If needed, tell about a time when you didn't give your child something he or she asked for because you knew it would not have been the best thing at the time.)

Journal

See page 43, part 2 of your journal.

Prayer

Gather around the prayer table. Light a candle, and say:

In our prayer today, we will take turns asking God for what we desire.
After each petition, we'll say together:
"Lord, on the day I called, you answered me."
Let us pray:
Jesus, you said "Ask, and you will receive."
We trust that you know what is best for us,
and we place our desires before you.

(Take turns saying "Lord, I ask for . . ." and make the response.)

Jesus, we now join together with you
to say the prayer you taught us.

Our Father, who art in heaven,
hallowed be thy name;
thy kingdom come;
thy will be done on earth
as it is in heaven.
Give us this day our daily bread;
and forgive us our trespasses
as we forgive those
who trespass against us;
and lead us not into temptation,
but deliver us from evil.
Amen.

Blessing

Share a hug or other sign of affection. Encourage your child to ask for help whenever it is needed.

Eighteenth Sunday in Ordinary Time

Recipe for Christian Living

Based on Luke 12:16 – 21

Opening Activity

Below is a recipe (also found in the child's journal on page 44) with one ingredient missing. When you discover the missing ingredient, add it to the recipe. (The answer is at the end of this session.)

Later, you may want to make the cookies and have someone over to enjoy them with you.

Chocolate Chip Cookies

2 cups shortening	2 teaspoons baking soda
1½ cups brown sugar	1 teaspoon salt
1½ cups white sugar	5 cups flour
4 eggs, beaten	2 teaspoons vanilla

Directions

Mix shortening and sugars. Cream until mixture is smooth. Add beaten eggs and blend well. Stir in dry ingredients. Add vanilla and missing ingredient. Drop walnut-size balls of dough onto ungreased cookie sheet. Bake in 350° F (175° C) oven for 8 to 10 minutes until done. Let cool 5 minutes before removing from the cookie sheet.

Journal

See page 44, part 1 of your journal.

Scripture

In today's gospel, Luke 12:16 – 21, Jesus tells us a parable, or story, about a man who is missing a very important ingredient in his life.

> A reading from the holy gospel according to Luke
>
> Jesus told the crowd this story:
>
> "A rich man's farm produced a big crop, and he said to himself, 'What can I do? I don't have a place large enough to store everything.'
>
> "Later, he said, 'Now I know what I'll do. I'll tear down my barns and build bigger ones, where I can store all my grain and other goods. Then I'll say to myself, "You have stored up enough good things to last for years to come. Live it up! Eat, drink, and enjoy yourself." '
>
> "But God said to him, 'You fool! Tonight you will die. Then who will get what you have stored up?'
>
> "This is what happens to people who store up everything for themselves, but are poor in the sight of God."
>
> The gospel of the Lord.

Reflection

What do you think this parable means? What do you think are the most important ingredients in your life?

Journal

See page 44, part 2 of your journal.

Prayer

Find things that represent important ingredients in your life (for example, pictures of family and friends, symbols of work or hobbies, reminders of faith), and place them on the prayer table. Then begin with:

God, giver of all gifts,
help us to remember that money and possessions
are only one part of our lives.
The richness of your love
is the most important ingredient.
We thank you for enriching our lives with _____ .

Lift each object as an offering and say what it represents (for example, hold up a family picture and say, "family love"; lift up a dollar bill or paycheck and say, "money for food, clothing and shelter").

We thank you for these
and all your blessings, in Jesus' name. Amen.

Blessing

Give each other a hug while saying:

(Name), you are an important ingredient in my life. May God bless you always.

Cookie Recipe's Missing Ingredient

12-ounce package chocolate chips

Nineteenth Sunday in Ordinary Time

Be Ready

Based on Luke 12:35–40

Opening Question

Have you ever missed something because you were not watching or weren't ready on time? For example, have you ever missed the bus because you slept late? Or has company ever come before you were ready? Tell about a time when you were not ready.

Journal

See page 45, part 1 of your journal.

Stories

Here are two stories about the importance of being watchful.

The Botched Dessert

"Nicole, would you make the pudding for tonight's dessert?" Mom said as she picked up her car keys and headed for the door. "I have a lot of errands to run, and that would be a big help to me."

"Sure, Mom," Nicole answered. She had made pudding lots of times.

Nicole got out the box of pudding mix, a gallon of milk, a large saucepan, a measuring cup and a wooden spoon. Then she read the directions on the back of the box, carefully measured the ingredients and put them into the pan. The directions on the box said "stir continuously," so Nicole put the pan on the burner, turned the knob to light the fire, and started to stir. She stirred and stirred for several minutes. Then she checked to be sure the burner was on. It was. "It should be boiling by now," she thought. She stirred some more, but still the mixture in the pan did not bubble.

Thinking that it would be a while longer before the pudding came to a boil, Nicole turned her back to the stove and went to the refrigerator to get something to drink. She pulled out a jar of apple juice, opened a cupboard to get a glass, carefully poured the juice, closed the jar and put it back in the fridge.

As she turned back to the stove, she could see that the pudding was boiling furiously. She put down the juice, picked up the wooden spoon and began stirring. She could tell that the mixture on the bottom of the pan was very thick, and as she stirred, black specks appeared in the pudding. It didn't smell exactly right either.

That night, Nicole hoped no one would notice anything wrong with the pudding. They were kind and didn't say anything, but she knew they could tell it had been scorched. Even Dad didn't finish his, and he usually asked for seconds on chocolate pudding!

"Next time," Nicole promised, "I'll stay with the pudding and keep stirring even if it takes all day."

The Morning It Snowed

"Wake up, boys!" Mom called from the bottom of the stairs. "Look out the window!"

Bryce slowly emerged from under the covers and stumbled to the window. His eyes opened wide.

"Kyle! You gotta see this."

Kyle made his way sleepily to the window, mumbling. Then he looked, too. Snow! In Southern California! Neither brother could remember the last time they had seen snow.

The two boys threw on jackets over their pajamas and dashed down the stairs and out the back door. Soon they were throwing snowballs and making snow angels. Mom laughed as she watched them through the window.

After a short time, Mom opened the door and called, "I'm going to leave for work a little early today. I'm sure that traffic will be a terrible mess with this snow. Come in and get ready for school." She saw Kyle head toward the house and then picked up her keys and went out the front door.

Just as Kyle reached the back door, Bryce let loose a big snowball that whacked Kyle on the neck.

"I'll get you for that," Kyle said, and retaliated with an even bigger snowball. The battle was on, and all thoughts of school were gone.

And then they heard it. They knew immediately it was the honking of their school bus. They raced to the front of the house. As their friends laughed and pointed, they realized they were still in their pajamas.

As they watched the school bus leave, Bryce moaned, "Now what'll we do?"

Talk About the Stories

How would you have felt at dessert time if you were Nicole?
What would you have done if you were Bryce or Kyle?

Scripture

Read Luke 12:35 – 40, and see what Jesus says about being watchful.

> A reading from the holy gospel according to Luke
>
> Jesus said to his disciples: "Be ready and keep your lamps burning just like those servants who wait up for their master to return from a wedding feast. As soon as he comes and knocks, they open the door for him.
>
> "Servants are fortunate if their master finds them awake and ready when he comes! I promise you that he will get ready and have his servants sit down so he can serve them. Those servants are really fortunate if their master finds them ready, even though he comes late at night or early in the morning.
>
> "You would surely not let a thief break into your home, if you knew when the thief was coming. So always be ready! You don't know when the Son of Man will come."
>
> The gospel of the Lord.

Reflection

Jesus used images from his culture so that the disciples could understand his messages. What images would Jesus use today to encourage us to be ready to welcome God into our lives?

Journal

See page 45, part 2 of your journal.

Prayer

If your circumstances allow, ask your child to open the front door as a sign that God is welcome in your home. Then pray:

O God of heaven and earth,
you are always welcome
in our hearts and in our home.
Help us to remember
your desire to be with us.
We ask this in Jesus' name. Amen.

Blessing

Place your hands on each other's heads, and say:

(Name), God desires to live with you forever.
You are blessed, in the name of the Father,
and of the Son, and of the Holy Spirit. Amen.

Twentieth Sunday in Ordinary Time

Stand Firm in Your Beliefs

Based on Luke 12:49–53

Opening Question

Do you know someone who stands up for his or her beliefs even when doing so is difficult or unpopular? Or maybe you have done this yourself. Talk about it.

Story

Here is a story about a young man who stood up for his beliefs. He lived many years ago but is still respected today by Christians all over the world.

Saint Francis of Assisi

Francis lived in Assisi, Italy, hundreds of years ago. He lived a life of ease, enjoying his parents' wealth. When he was about twenty years old, something happened to change all that.

He fought in a battle and was a prisoner of war for a year. When he returned home, he became seriously ill. Being sick made Francis see things differently. He gave up all his wealth and started to help the poor and the sick. Francis' father did not like his son's new life one bit. He insisted that Francis come back home and work in the family business selling cloth. But Francis knew that God wanted something different. Francis listened to God and continued to live like the poor people.

This enraged his father so much that he disowned Francis. He refused to give Francis love and support. With nothing of his own to share, Francis began to beg for food and share it with the poor. Francis was not popular at first. Even some of the young children threw stones at him when he came into the village to find food. But he kept sharing his food each day. Soon two other young men followed his example. Then more and more men and women left their comfortable homes and joined Francis in living a life devoted to prayer and helping the poor.

Before Francis died, more than 3,000 people were members of the Franciscan Order, which he had started.

Talk About the Story

Pick out one of the situations in the story and tell how you would have felt if you were Francis.

Scripture

Jesus tells us that it is not always easy to stand up for what we believe. Sometimes it brings disagreements. Read Luke 12:49–53.

A reading from the holy gospel according to Luke

Jesus said to his disciples: "I came to set fire to the earth, and I surely wish it were already on fire!
"I am going to be put to a hard test. And I will have to suffer a lot of pain until it is over.

"Do you think that I came to bring peace to earth? No indeed! I came to make people choose sides. A family of five will be divided, with two of them against the other three. Fathers and sons will turn against one another, and mothers and daughters will do the same. Mothers-in-law and daughters-in-law will also turn against each other."

The gospel of the Lord.

Reflection

What did you hear Jesus say in this passage? When might it be difficult to stand up for God's ways?

Journal

See page 46 of your journal.

Prayer

On a large sheet of paper, have family members write down values that are important to them. Place the paper on the prayer table, and pray:

Jesus, you know what it is like
to stand up for values
that are not always popular.
It cost you your life.
Help us to stand up for our values.

Read from the paper on the prayer table.

Please give us courage to be your disciples
forever and ever. Amen.

Blessing

Bless each other, saying:

(Name), may God give you courage to be a disciple,
in the name of the Father,
and of the Son,
and of the Holy Spirit. Amen.

Twenty-first Sunday in Ordinary Time

A Second Look at Discipleship

Based on Luke 13:22–30

Opening Activity

Have your child turn to page 47, part 1 of the journal, or use the picture below.
Is this man smiling or frowning?

Is he bald? Does he have a beard?
Now take a second look. Turn the page upside down. What do you see?
Have you ever thought something would be easy to do, and then, after taking a second look at it, found it to be harder than you expected? Talk about it. (Parent, see page 47, part 1 of the adult journal.)

Scripture

Who do you think are the modern followers of Jesus?
Some people thought it would be easy to follow Jesus. In Luke 13:22–30, Jesus uses parables, or stories, that help us take a second look at what it means to be a faithful disciple.

A reading from the holy gospel according to Luke

As Jesus was on his way to Jerusalem, he taught the people in the towns and villages. Someone asked him, "Lord, are only a few people going to be saved?"

Jesus answered: "Do all you can to go in by the narrow door! A lot of people will try to get in, but will not be able to. Once the owner of the house gets up and locks the door, you will be left standing outside. You will knock on the door and say, 'Sir, open the door for us!'

"But the owner will answer, 'I don't know a thing about you!'

"Then you will start saying, 'We dined with you, and you taught in our streets.'

"But he will say, 'I really don't know who you are! Get away from me all you evil people!'

"Then when you have been thrown outside, you will weep and grit your teeth because you will see Abraham and Isaac and all the prophets in God's kingdom. People will come from all directions and sit down to feast in God's kingdom. There the ones who are now least important will be the most important, and those who are now most important will be the least important."

The gospel of the Lord.

Reflection

Close your eyes, and in your mind, picture a modern group of Jesus' followers. Whom do you see? *(Pause 10–20 seconds.)* Reread or think about the scripture. Now take a second look. Who is in the group this time? Are you there? *(Pause 10–20 seconds.)* Is there someone there who might surprise the others? *(Pause 10–20 seconds.)* Talk about your reflection.

Journal

See page 47, part 2 of your journal.

Prayer

On the prayer table, place the journals with magazine or newspaper pictures of people doing something positive to help build God's kingdom. Include your own family pictures. Ask the child to lift up the journals or pictures in offering as you pray:

God, help us to follow Jesus
as we build your kingdom here on earth.
It is not always easy to be a disciple,
because discipleship calls for sacrifice.
We lift up all your followers in Jesus' name. Amen.

Blessing

Bless each other with oil, saying:

(Name), disciple of Jesus,
may God bless you with courage.
In the name of the Father,
and of the Son,
and of the Holy Spirit. Amen.

Twenty-second Sunday in Ordinary Time

Who Shall Be First?

Based on Luke 14:1, 7 – 14

Opening Question

When you are in a lunch line, do you like to be first or last? When are some times you like to be first? When do you like to be last?

Story

Kristen's Choice

Kristen was already home from school when her Mom and Dad returned from their Florida vacation. Both Kristen and her sister, Bridget, had asked their parents for Mickey Mouse watches. After hearing about the highlights of their trip, Kristen asked her Mom, "Did you bring me and Bridget anything?" Mom smiled and handed Kristen a bag with Mickey Mouse's face on it. Inside were two watches — one had a blue band, the other, red.

"Kristen, you get to choose first. Do you want the red watch or the blue one?" her mother asked.

"Mom, let's wait for Bridget. I like the red one, but I know that's Bridget's favorite color. When she gets home, maybe we can flip a coin for the first choice."

Talk About the Story

What do you think of Kristen's response? Later, Kristen and Bridget talked about the watches. How do you think they felt? What do you think they said to each other?

Journal

See page 48, part 1 of your journal.

Scripture

Kristen and Bridget would like today's scripture reading. In Luke 14:1, 7 – 14, Jesus talks about the advantage of being last.

> A reading from the holy gospel according to Luke

> One Sabbath Jesus was having dinner in the home of an important Pharisee, and everyone was carefully watching Jesus.
>
> Jesus saw how the guests had tried to take the best seats. So he told them: "When you are invited to a wedding feast, don't sit in the best place. Someone more important may have been invited. Then the one who invited you will come and say, 'Give your place to this other guest!' You will be embarrassed and will have to sit in the worst place.

"When you are invited to be a guest, go and sit in the worst place. Then the one who invited you may come and say, 'My friend, take a better seat!' You will then be honored in front of all the other guests. If you put yourself above others, you will be put down. But if you humble yourself, you will be honored."

Then Jesus said to the man who invited him: "When you give a dinner or a banquet, don't invite your friends and family and relatives and rich neighbors. If you do, they will invite you in return, and you will be paid back. When you give a feast, invite the poor, the crippled, the lame, and the blind. They cannot pay you back. But God will bless you and reward you when his people rise from death."

The gospel of the Lord.

Reflection

Imagine you are at the banquet with Jesus. Where are you sitting? What do you hear Jesus say?

Journal

See page 48, part 2 of your journal.

Prayer and Blessing

If possible, share a meal or treat together. Before eating, pray:

God, great provider and gift-giver,
thank you for nourishing our family
with so many gifts.
Help us to nourish each other
with honor and respect,
as the gospel teaches us.

Make a sign of the cross over the family and food, praying:

Bless us and these gifts of food in Jesus' name. Amen.

Twenty-third Sunday in Ordinary Time

The Cost of Discipleship

Based on Luke 14:25–27

Opening Activity

Today's gospel continues the theme of discipleship. You may want to read or reread the story of Saint Francis of Assisi on page 113, or you may want to do the activity in your journal on page 49, part 1. Both activities will help create an understanding of the cost of discipleship.

Discussion

If you read the story of Saint Francis, ask: What did it cost Francis to do what he believed? If you did the journal activity, ask: What did you decide about your project? (Parent: Be sure to share your journal project, too.)

Scripture

Jesus wanted the crowd to decide what they would be willing to do to be his followers. Read Luke 14:25–27.

> A reading from the holy gospel according to Luke
>
> Large crowds were walking along with Jesus, when he turned and said:
> "You cannot be my disciple unless you love me more than you love your father and mother, your wife and children, and your brothers and sisters. You cannot come with me unless you love me more than you love your own life.
> "You cannot be my disciple unless you carry your own cross and come with me."
>
> The gospel of the Lord.

Reflection

What did you hear Jesus say about being a disciple? What are some sacrifices you have made recently that show you are a disciple of Jesus?

Journal

See page 49, part 2 of your journal.

Prayer

Place a cross on the prayer table, and begin:

Jesus, you have called us
to be your disciples.
You ask us to look
at what discipleship will cost us.
Give us the courage
to take up our crosses
and to help others
carry their crosses, too.
You are our God, forever and ever. Amen.

Blessing

Take the cross from the prayer table, and present it to each person, saying:

(Name), God gives you strength to carry your cross and follow Jesus. I, too, am willing to help you carry your cross. In the name of the Father, and of the Son, and of the Holy Spirit. Amen.

Twenty-fourth Sunday in Ordinary Time

The Joy of a Mended Relationship

Based on Luke 15:11–32

Opening Question

How do you feel when you mend a relationship or make up after a disagreement?

Scripture

In Luke 15:11–32, Jesus tells a story about a relationship that needed mending. Act out this play to see what happened. If your family is small, you may need to take more than one part. Characters: narrator, father, younger son, older son, servant.

A Mended Relationship

Narrator	A man had two sons. The younger son said to his father,
Younger son	Give me my share of the property.
Narrator	So the father divided his property between his two sons. Not long after that, the younger son packed up everything he owned and left for a foreign country, where he wasted all his money in wild living. He had spent everything, when a bad famine spread through that whole land. Soon he had nothing to eat. He went to work for a man in that country, and the man sent him out to take care of his pigs. He would have been glad to eat what the pigs were eating, but no one gave him a thing. Finally, he came to his senses and said:
Younger son	My father's workers have plenty to eat, and here I am, starving to death! I will leave and go to my father and say to him, "Father, I have sinned against God in heaven and against you. I am no longer good enough to be called your son. Treat me like one of your workers."
Narrator	The younger son got up and started back to his father. But when he was still a long way off, his father saw him and felt sorry for him. He ran to his son and hugged and kissed him. The son said:
Younger son	Father, I have sinned against God in heaven and against you. I am no longer good enough to be called your son.
Narrator	But his father said to the servants:
Father	Hurry and bring the best clothes and put them on him. Give him a ring for his finger and sandals for his feet. Get the best calf and prepare it, so we can eat and celebrate. This son of mine was dead, but he has now come back to life. He was lost and has now been found.

Narrator	And they began to celebrate. The older son had been out in the field, but when he came near the house, he heard the music and dancing. So he called one of the servants over and asked,
Older son	What's going on here?
Servant	Your brother has come home safe and sound, and your father ordered us to kill the best calf.
Narrator	The older brother got so mad that he would not even go into the house. His father came out and begged him to go in. But he said to his father,
Older son	For years I have worked for you like a slave and have always obeyed you. But you have never even given me a little goat, so that I could give a dinner for my friends. This other son of yours wasted your money on bad women. And now that he has come home, you ordered the best calf to be killed for a feast.
Father	My son, you are always with me, and everything I have is yours. But we should be glad and celebrate! Your brother was dead, but he is now alive. He was lost and has now been found.

Reflection

Take turns finishing the following sentences:

If I were the father, I _____ .

If I were the younger son, I _____ .

If I were the older brother, I _____ .

Journal

See page 50 of your journal.

Prayer

Loving God,
we stand before you today
knowing that you always accept us with joy.
Give us the courage to forgive
and to rejoice over our mended relationships.
We ask this through Jesus,
who came to mend the whole world. Amen.

Blessing

Give each other a hug, saying one of the following or something similar.

- May the joy of Christ fill your heart.
- May the peace of Christ be with you.
- I am sorry if I hurt you.
- *Other* _____ .

Twenty-fifth Sunday in Ordinary Time

Jesus Asks Us to Share

Based on Luke 16:10–13

Opening Question

If you had a thousand dollars, how would you spend it? Make a list. After doing today's journal activity, you might have another idea to add to your list.

Journal

See page 51, part 1 of your journal.

Scripture

Read Luke 16:10–13 to find out what Jesus says about the use of money.

> **A reading from the holy gospel according to Luke**
>
> Jesus said to his disciples: "Anyone who can be trusted in little matters can also be trusted in important matters. But anyone who is dishonest in little matters will be dishonest in important matters. If you cannot be trusted with this wicked wealth, who will trust you with true wealth? And if you cannot be trusted with what belongs to someone else, who will give you something that will be your own?
>
> "You cannot be the slave of two masters. You will like one more than the other or be more loyal to one than to the other. You cannot serve God and money."
>
> **The gospel of the Lord.**

Reflection

What did you hear Jesus say?

Optional Activity

Choose one or both of the following:

1. Ask your child what the statement "You cannot give yourself to God and money" means. This might be a good time to talk to your child about church support and other charities in the community.

2. If your child gets an allowance or has money of his or her own, invite the child to decide how much of this money might be shared with others. Put the donation into a bowl, which can be placed on the prayer table. Add your contribution also. As a family, decide to whom you will give the money.

Journal

See page 51, part 2 of your journal.

Prayer and Blessing

Bless the family (and the contributions if you chose activity 2) with blessed or tap water, saying:

Just and generous God,
you have entrusted the wealth of the earth
to your people.
Help us to share our gifts
and to have an open heart
to receive from others
when we are in need.
We ask this through Jesus,
who calls us to share. Amen.

Twenty-sixth Sunday in Ordinary Time

Sharing Our Gifts

Based on Luke 16:19–31

Opening Question

Discuss one or more of the following:

- Was there ever a time when someone ignored you or didn't take care of your needs? (Parent and child both share stories.)
- How would you feel if you were asked to share something new with a brother, sister or friend?
- How would you feel if you used your savings to buy food for a poor family?
- How do you feel when someone you don't like comes for a visit?
- How do you feel when you refuse to be friends with someone?
- How do you feel when you share gifts with your family at Christmas?

Journal

See page 52, part 1 of your journal.

Story

Here is a story about someone who is not happy. Read to see how she handles the situation.

A Gift to Share

"Never will I call Julie 'mother,'" Heather promised her reflection in the oval mirror. "Thanksgiving week is turning out all wrong. I've only been here two days, and all Dad talks about is Julie. I may as well go back home." With each thought, she brushed her shiny hair harder, until the brush accidentally banged against her dresser top. The delicate glass angel carrying a sign, "Welcome, Heather," lay in pieces on the varnished floor of the bedroom. Heather flinched. Her new stepmother had just given it to her yesterday. But then bitter thoughts returned. "Who cares? She's only trying to buy me off anyway."

"Heather, come sing for Julie," her father called from the living room. "Did you know that she was once a professional blues singer?"

In the mirror, Heather could see her father sitting on the maroon leather sofa stroking her stepmother's black curly hair.

"Call Julie 'mother.' Sing for Julie." Heather gritted her teeth. "I won't do it. I hate her for taking Dad away."

She coughed noisily. "Dad, I can't," she lied. "I'm getting a sore throat."

She saw Julie immediately rise and come to her door. "Let's get some lozenges for your throat. I hope your voice will be in shape for the concert in Boston next week," Julie said. Heather sighed and followed her stepmother into the next room. She was tired. It was hard work hating someone who was so nice.

Her father's bedroom looked different. The curtains were blue, and a framed baby picture replaced the deer head that once stood on the fireplace mantel.

"How beautiful," Heather said to herself, admiring the smooth brown skin of the infant in the picture. In a tiny fist the baby was clutching a pacifier. "Is that your baby?" Heather asked. Before Julie could even answer, Heather continued, "Why don't you even live with your own child?" Her voice was nasty and accusing as she looked her stepmother squarely in the eyes.

"That's Nelson," Julie replied sadly. "He died three years ago. Shortly afterward my husband, Carl, left me and asked for a divorce. Eventually our marriage was annulled. It still isn't easy for me to talk about."

Heather studied the picture and her stepmother's sad face. "How can I hate Julie now?" she asked herself, feeling defeated. "What difference does it make?" she thought. "Dad doesn't care for me anymore, now that he's got her."

"I suppose it wasn't your fault that Dad did this to me," she said out loud, her voice flat and discouraged.

"What did your Dad do?" her stepmother asked, puzzled.

"Got married. It's not the same. Dad likes you better. Uncle Harry and Aunt Carolyn have been nice since mother died, but they have their own kids. I only had one parent and now I don't have any," said Heather.

"I don't know who is first or second, Heather, but I do know that your Dad loves you. He talks about you constantly."

Heather's eyes widened. Her heart beat faster. Julie laid the lozenges down on the small table next to the oak bed.

"Heather, I don't think you need anything for your throat. I think it's your heart that is hurting." She opened her arms.

Without stopping to hate or even to argue with herself, Healther walked right into those open arms. To her surprise, she felt warm and comforted.

"Your father wants everything to go well between you and me, but he isn't always realistic. You don't have to sing, and you don't have to call me 'mother.' But you can have two parents again, if you wish."

Healther hadn't thought of that. After a few moments of silence, she said, "Julie, will you sing a blues song for me tonight? And, if you'd like, I could sing the song I've been practicing for the concert."

When Julie smiled, it made Heather wonder, "What would it be like to call Julie 'mother'?"

Talk About the Story

When have you ever felt like Heather? or Julie?
Finish this sentence: If I were Heather, I _____ .

Scripture

Today's story is about someone whose heart was cold because he refused to love and care for another. Read Luke 16:19–31.

A reading from the holy gospel according to Luke

Jesus told his disciples this story: "There was once a rich man who wore expensive clothes and every day ate the best food. But a poor beggar named Lazarus was brought to the gate of the rich man's house. He was happy just to eat the scraps that fell from the rich man's table.

"His body was covered with sores, and dogs kept coming up to lick them. The poor man died, and angels took him to the place of honor next to Abraham.

"The rich man also died and was buried. He went to hell and was suffering terribly. When he looked up and saw Abraham far off and Lazarus at his side, he said to Abraham, 'Have pity on me! Send Lazarus to dip his finger in water and touch my tongue. I'm suffering terribly in this fire.'

"Abraham answered, 'My friend, remember that while you lived, you had everything good, and Lazarus had everything bad. Now he is happy, and you are in pain. And besides, there is a deep ditch between us, and no one from either side can cross over.'

"But the rich man said, 'Abraham, then please send Lazarus to my father's home. Let him warn my five brothers, so they won't come to this horrible place.'

"Abraham answered, 'Your brothers can read what Moses and the prophets wrote. They should pay attention to that.'

"Then the rich man said, 'No, that's not enough! If only someone from the dead would go to them, they would listen and turn to God.'

"So Abraham said, 'If they won't pay attention to Moses and the prophets, they won't listen even to someone who comes back from the dead.' "

The gospel of the Lord.

Reflection

As you share this scripture with your child, focus on the joy of giving rather than on threats of punishment or hell. Then retell the gospel, making a happy ending for everyone in the story.

Optional Activity

Choose one or more of the following activities to do with your child.

- Take a ride to a poor district in town. Then discuss how you might adopt a family for Christmas.
- Help at a soup kitchen.
- Have your child call the local food pantry and ask what items are needed for the hungry. Go shopping together and deliver the food to the food pantry. Or help stock the shelves.
- Plan, prepare and deliver a meal to someone who is sick or grieving.
- Phone or write a letter to a relative who could use a little cheering up.

Journal

See page 52, part 2 of your journal.

Prayer

Place a pretty container of oil and your journals on the prayer table, and pray:

Generous God,
you have given us so much
because you love us.
Open our hearts
to share our possessions, talents,
time and friendship,
even when it is hard.

Twenty-sixth Sunday in Ordinary Time

Ask your child to hold up the journals, and continue:
All-giving God,
we offer to you and to your people
these gifts we have to share,
in the name of your Son, Jesus. Amen.

Blessing

Take the oil and bless each other's hands, saying:

(Name), may God, the most generous gift-giver of all,
bless your hands as you give to others.
In the name of the Father,
and of the Son,
and of the Holy Spirit. Amen.

Twenty-seventh Sunday in Ordinary Time

Lord, Increase Our Faith

Based on Luke 17:5–10

Opening Question and Activity

What kind of things do you believe in? (For example, in keeping your word, in friendship.)

On page 165 in the supplement you will find words that express a value or an idea. Together, play the "I Believe Game."

Scripture, Part 1

To have faith means to believe. Today's scripture has two parts to it. Read the first part, Luke 17:5–6, and see what Jesus says about faith.

> A reading from the holy gospel according to Luke
>
> The apostles said to the Lord, "Make our faith stronger!"
> Jesus replied: "If you had faith no bigger than a tiny mustard seed, you could tell this mulberry tree to pull itself up, roots and all, and to plant itself in the ocean. And it would!"

Reflection

If you have some mustard seed in your spice rack, show your child how small the seed is. Explain that the seed, with God's help, has the possibility of growing into a tree. Our faith can grow with God's help, too. Tell a story of how your faith sustained you in a situation that seemed impossible.

Scripture, Part 2

In the "I Believe Game," you spoke about the values you believe in as a Christian. Read the second part of today's gospel, Luke 17:7–10, and see what Jesus expects of a good servant or Christian.

> A reading from the holy gospel according to Luke
>
> "If your servant comes in from plowing or from taking care of the sheep, would you say, 'Welcome! Come on in and have something to eat'? No, you wouldn't say that. You would say, 'Fix me something to eat. Get ready to serve me, so I can have my meal. Then later on you can eat and drink.'
>
> "Servants don't deserve special thanks for doing what they are supposed to do. And that's how it should be with you. When you've done all you should, then say, 'We are merely servants, and we have simply done our duty.'"
>
> The gospel of the Lord.

Reflection

What would it be like to be the good servant Jesus is talking about?

Journal

See page 53 of your journal.

Prayer

Explain that today's prayer is the Creed that we say at Mass. Say it together with your child. Also, if you have a mustard seed, place it on the prayer table.

We believe in one God,
    the Father, the Almighty,
    maker of heaven and earth,
    of all that is seen and unseen.
We believe in one Lord, Jesus Christ,
    the only Son of God,
    eternally begotten of the Father,
    God from God, Light from Light,
    true God from true God,
    begotten, not made, one in Being with the Father.
    Through him all things were made.
    For us and for our salvation he came down from heaven:
    by the power of the Holy Spirit he was born of the Virgin Mary,
        and became man.
    For our sake he was crucified under Pontius Pilate;
    he suffered, died, and was buried.
    On the third day he rose again in fulfillment of the Scriptures;
    he ascended into heaven and is seated
        at the right hand of the Father.
    He will come again in glory to judge the living and the dead,
        and his kingdom will have no end.
We believe in the Holy Spirit, the Lord, the giver of life,
    who proceeds from the Father and the Son.
    With the Father and the Son he is worshiped and glorified.
    He has spoken through the Prophets.
    We believe in one holy catholic and apostolic Church.
    We acknowledge one baptism for the forgiveness of sins.
    We look for the resurrection of the dead,
        and the life of the world to come.
    Amen.

Blessing

Bless each other, saying:

(Name), may your faith increase.
In the name of the Father, and of the Son, and of the Holy Spirit. Amen.

Twenty-eighth Sunday in Ordinary Time

Thank You, God

Based on Luke 17:11–19

Opening Activity

Choose one or more of the following activities:

- Print the words MAIL, AUNT EDNA, GIFT, JESSIE and THANK YOU on a large sheet of paper. Put the paper where everyone can see it. Together, make up a story that includes these five words. Each person takes a turn, adding a sentence until the story is complete.
- Write a thank-you note together for a gift the family has received.
- Talk about how you felt when someone thanked you recently.

Journal

See page 54, part 1 of your journal.

Scripture

Read Luke 17:11–19 to see what Jesus says about gratitude.

> **A reading from the holy gospel according to Luke**
>
> On his way to Jerusalem, Jesus went along the border between Samaria and Galilee. As he was going into a village, ten men with leprosy came toward him. They stood at a distance and shouted, "Jesus, Master, have pity on us!"
>
> Jesus looked at them and said, "Go show yourselves to the priests." On their way they were healed. When one of them discovered that he was healed, he came back, shouting praises to God. He bowed down at the feet of Jesus and thanked him. The man was from the country of Samaria.
>
> Jesus asked, "Weren't ten men healed? Where are the other nine? Why was this foreigner the only one who came back to thank God?"
>
> Then Jesus told the man, "You may get up and go. Your faith has made you well."
>
> **The gospel of the Lord.**

Reflection

Imagine you were Jesus, one of the lepers or a bystander. How would you have felt?

Journal

See page 54, part 2 of your journal.

Prayer

Bring your journals to the prayer table. Take turns mentioning a gift listed in the journal. After each gift, say together: "Thank you, God." For example:

Person 1: **For Grandpa.**
All: **Thank you, God.**

Blessing

Bless each other on the forehead or with a hug, saying:
Thank you, God, for *(Name)*.
May she or he be blessed in your name forever and ever. Amen.

Twenty-ninth Sunday in Ordinary Time

Keep Praying

Based on Luke 18:1–8

Opening Question

Have you ever asked more than once for something that you really wanted? Tell about it.

Story

Here is a tale about perseverance in asking for something. Perserverance means not giving up when obstacles get in the way.

Sammy Centipede's Search For Socks

From a crevice in the sidewalk, Sammy Centipede watched flecks of snow float down from the gray sky overhead. Though his tan coat covered him, his legs quaked from the chill of the brisk November wind.

"I should have stayed inside like a sensible house centipede," Sammy chided himself. Then he quickly added, "And miss this view of the world? Never! I will find a way." A child skipped toward him. Sammy noticed the girl's fiery red socks. "Socks! That's what I need," Sammy exclaimed, "socks for my many and chilly legs." He braved the wind and began his search.

Feeling the wind whipping about his legs, he slithered under the door of a telephone booth. Inside, away from the cold, he was able to think. "Where can I find socks?" he asked himself over and over. In the corner lay a page from the phone book, crumbled and dirty.

Sammy crawled into a fold for more warmth. When he looked down, he saw an ad in clear, large print.

MR. LARAMIE'S SOCKS
SOCKS FOR ALL
SHORT OR TALL

At the bottom in fine print was an address. Sammy squinted at it, then shouted, "It's right down the street! I will ask Mr. Laramie for help."

Scurrying onto the street, he moved rapidly until he reached the entrance of the huge store. Attaching himself to a customer's trouser leg, Sammy entered through a revolving door.

"May I talk to Mr. Laramie? I need socks for my many and chilly legs," he asked a clerk.

"Eeek! A centipede!" screamed the man, leaping onto a ledge. Dozens of red and black socks tumbled to the floor.

Sammy slipped under the toe of a red sock and waited. A woman approached. Sammy stepped out cautiously, two legs at a time, and repeated his question. "May I talk with Mr. Laramie, please? I need socks for my many and chilly legs, which will surely freeze during this long and cold winter if I don't protect them."

The clerk snickered, "We don't carry centipede socks anymore, what with all the clamor for leggings."

"You don't have to get sarcastic," Sammy thought. He again asked, "May I talk to Mr. Laramie?"

"He's too busy to talk to a — ugh — centipede," the woman said disdainfully.

"Too busy, too busy," Sammy heard again and again. But he wouldn't give up. He knew Mr. Laramie would help him. Didn't the advertisement say, "Socks for all, short or tall"?

Sammy crawled into a crack in the floor and waited. As the grandfather clock struck ten, he saw and heard a great bowing and scraping in the rear of the store. "Good morning, Mr. Laramie. Good morning, Mr. Laramie." Everyone was gathering around a dignified gentleman. Sammy's heart beat faster as he raced to the scene of the clamor.

"There's that pesky centipede again," someone screamed. "Get him!"

Sammy tried to scoot away, but he was blocked by an enormous foot. Looking up, he saw Mr. Laramie leaning down and smiling at him.

"My good centipede, what can Laramie's do for you today?"

"I need socks, winter socks for my many and chilly legs," Sammy said hopefully.

"I see, I see," the man said, pondering this unusual request. Then he summoned his employees before him, "Search the storeroom for socks for the centipede!"

"Did he say, 'a pox on the centipede'?" one clerk asked.

"No, hee, hee" another laughed. "I think he said, 'Find socks for the centipede.'"

"Hee, hee, ha, ha, ho, ho," others echoed.

Mr. Laramie glared and repeated, "Search the storeroom for socks for the centipede."

No one stirred. Had Mr. Laramie gone over the edge? Should they humor him or ignore the command?

This time Mr. Laramie roared, "Search the storeroom for socks for the centipede. Pronto! A.S.A.P.! Move!"

Everyone scattered. A hustle and bustle came from the direction of the storeroom. Sammy heard boxes being opened. Boxes being closed. Boxes being moved forward. Boxes being moved back.

Finally, Mr. Laramie himself entered the storeroom. Moments later he emerged, holding an elegant box marked "Centipede socks, winter." "Will these do?" he asked Sammy.

"Yes, sir!" Sammy exclaimed.

Then he climbed right into the box and fitted the socks one at a time, until all of his many and chilly legs were warm.

Talk About the Story

If you were Sammy, do you think you would have given up or persevered?

Scripture

Jesus tells a parable, or story, about perseverance. Read Luke 18:1 – 8 to see what Jesus says about not giving up on God.

A reading from the holy gospel according to Luke

Jesus told his disciples a story about how they should keep on praying and never give up:

"In a town there was once a judge who didn't fear God or care about people. In that same town there was a widow who kept going to the judge and saying, 'Make sure that I get fair treatment in court.'

"For a while the judge refused to do anything. Finally, he said to himself, 'Even though I don't fear God or care about people, I will help this widow because she keeps on bothering me. If I don't help her, she will wear me out.'"

The Lord said: "Think about what the crooked judge said. Won't God protect his chosen ones who pray to him day and night? Won't he be concerned for them? He will surely hurry and help them. But when the Son of Man comes, will he find on this earth anyone with faith?"

The gospel of the Lord.

Reflection

What did you hear in the scripture? When might a parent not give a child something that he or she keeps asking for? Does God answer every prayer? (Parent: You might tell your child that God hears every prayer, but because God is wiser than we are, we don't always get what we want.)

Journal

See page 55 of your journal.

Prayer

Gather around the prayer table, light a candle, and pray:

God, you are like a generous parent
who cares for our needs.
We know that in your wisdom
you will give us what is best.
Help us to trust that you hear us
and that you answer us when we pray.
We ask this through Jesus, your Son. Amen.

Blessing

Bless your child with a hug and/or the sign of the cross, saying:

(Name), I love you, and I always want to know what you want. May God help me to do what is best for you at this time in your life.

Let us bless each other, in the name of the Father, and of the Son, and of the Holy Spirit. Amen.

Thirtieth Sunday in Ordinary Time

Who Is Pleasing to God?

Based on Luke 18:9 – 14

Opening Question

Which of these people would you like to have as a friend? Tell why.

Andy   "Hi, John! Look at my new ten-speed bike. I bet I can ride faster than you can on your old bike."

Burt   "Dad and I are building a tree house. Would you like to help us? We can have our club meetings in there."

Mary   "My sister and I made some cookies. Would you like some?"

Tess   "You just got a C on your test? I had five A's this week. I bet I'm the smartest one in the whole school."

Scripture

Jesus has some ideas about people like Andy, Burt, Mary and Tess. Read Luke 18:9 – 14.

> A reading from the holy gospel according to Luke

> Jesus told a story to some people who thought they were better than others and who looked down on everyone else:
>   "Two men went into the temple to pray. One was a Pharisee and the other a tax collector.
>   "The Pharisee stood over by himself and prayed, 'God, I thank you that I am not greedy dishonest, and unfaithful in marriage like other people. And I am really glad that I am not like that tax collector over there. I go without eating for two days a week, and I give you one tenth of all I earn.'
>   "The tax collector stood off at a distance and did not think he was good enough even to look up toward heaven. He was so sorry for what he had done that he pounded his chest and prayed, 'God, have pity on me. I am such a sinner.'"
>   Then Jesus said, "When the two men went home, it was the tax collector and not the Pharisee who was pleasing to God. If you put yourself above others, you will be put down. But if you humble yourself, you will be honored."

> The gospel of the Lord.

Reflection

When have you felt like the Pharisee? the tax collector? You may want to explain these sayings: "Pride goes before the fall"; "the humble will be exalted." This might be a good time to talk about self-esteem. We have good self-esteem when we acknowledge our gifts and know that they come from God. Christians use their gifts to bring joy to others.

Journal

See page 56 of your journal.

Prayer

Have each person bring something to the prayer table that represents a gift received from God (for example, a baseball, a sheet of music, a book or a family picture). At the appropriate time, invite each person to lift the object in offering and thank God for that particular gift, saying something similar to the following:

- *Lift baseball:* Thank you, God, for the talent to be an athlete.
- *Lift sheet of music:* Thank you, God, for my musical talent.
- *Lift book:* Thank you, God, for the joy of reading.
- *Lift family picture:* Thank you, God, for my wonderful family.

Begin with:

Generous God, you fill us with many great gifts.
Today we honor you by using the gifts
You have given us.

Invite each person to lift the object brought to the prayer table and to thank God for it.

Continue:

Help us not to brag about our gifts
but to share them.
We ask this through Jesus,
who shared the gift of his life with us. Amen.

Blessing

Bless each other by saying:

(Name), may you find many ways to share your gifts.
In the name of the Father, and of the Son,
and of the Holy Spirit. Amen.

THIRTY-FIRST SUNDAY IN ORDINARY TIME

Jesus Sees the Good in Everyone

Based on Luke 19:1 – 10

Opening Activity

How many treasures can you find in this picture?

Talk About the Picture

People are like the picture above. If you look hard enough, you can discover treasures hidden in each person. What treasures have you discovered in each member of your family?

    If other family members are present, remind them to make only positive comments about each other. On separate pieces of paper, write each person's name and the "treasures" mentioned. Place these on the prayer table.

Scripture

Read Luke 19:1 – 10 and discover how Jesus found the treasure in a person whom no one liked.

A reading from the holy gospel according to Luke

Jesus was going through Jericho, where a man named Zacchaeus lived. He was in charge of collecting taxes and was very rich.

Jesus was heading his way, and Zacchaeus wanted to see what he was like. But Zacchaeus was a short man and could not see over the crowd. So he ran ahead and climbed up into a sycamore tree. When Jesus got there, he looked up and said, "Zacchaeus, hurry down! I want to stay with you today."

Zacchaeus hurried down and gladly welcomed Jesus.

Everyone who saw this started grumbling, "This man Zacchaeus is a sinner! And Jesus is going home to eat with him."

Later that day Zacchaeus stood up and said to the Lord, "I will give half of my property to the poor. And I will now pay back four times as much to everyone I have ever cheated."

Jesus said to Zacchaeus, "Today you and your family have been saved, because you are a true son of Abraham. The Son of Man came to look for and to save people who are lost."

The gospel of the Lord.

Reflection

If you were Zacchaeus, what would you see? What would you hear?
How would you feel?

Journal

See page 57 of your journal.

Prayer Blessing

Place the "treasure" papers and a lighted candle on the prayer table. When it is a person's turn to hold the candle, place your hand on that person's shoulder. If others are present, invite them to do the same while the blessing is prayed.

As each person is presented with the candle, say:

(Name), the light of Christ is with you.

Place hands on the shoulder of the one holding the candle.

Thank you, God, for (Name), a treasured member of our family.

All respond: **Amen.**

Thirty-first Sunday in Ordinary Time

Thirty-second Sunday in Ordinary Time

Life Everlasting

Based on Luke 20:27 – 38

Opening Questions and Activities

What do you think you will be doing 100 years from now? Has someone close to you died? What do you think they are doing? (Parent, see page 58, part 1 of the adult journal.)

(Optional) Think about the trees that have lost their leaves. They look dead, but in spring you will notice little green buds on the branches. Those buds will grow into leaves, and the tree will look alive again because life is in the tree all year long. Winter and spring are like our own death and resurrection. Our bodies die but we are born into a new life with God, angels and all of our family and friends who have gone before us.

(Optional) This might be a good time to plant tulip or iris bulbs with your child. Explain that the bulbs contains life and that in the spring a beautiful flower will appear.

(Optional) Your child may have had science classes about the developmental stages of a Monarch butterfly. (See page 58, part 1 of the child's journal.) Ask your child to explain the various stages. Then compare these stages to our death and resurrection.

Scripture

In Jesus' time, a group of people called the Sadducees did not believe in life after death. They tried to trap Jesus into seeing things their way. Read Luke 20:27 – 38 to see what Jesus says.

A reading from the holy gospel according to Luke

The Sadducees did not believe that people would rise to life after death. So some of them came to Jesus and said:

"Teacher, Moses wrote that if a married man dies and has no children, his brother should marry the widow. Their first son would then be thought of as the son of the dead brother.

"There were once seven brothers. The first one married, but died without having any children. The second one married his brother's widow, and he also died without having any children. The same thing happened to the third one.

"Finally, all seven brothers married that woman and died without having any children. At last the woman died.

"When God raises people from death, whose wife will this woman be? All seven brothers had married her."

Jesus answered: "The people in this world get married. But in the future world no one who is worthy to rise from death will either marry or die. They will be like the angels and will be God's children, because they have been raised to life.

"In the story about the burning bush, Moses clearly shows that people will live again. He said, 'The Lord is the God worshiped by Abraham, Isaac and Jacob.' So the Lord is not the God of the dead, but of the living. This means that anyone is alive as far as God is concerned."

The gospel of the Lord.

Reflection

Like the Sadducees, some people do not believe in the resurrection or in life after death. What would you tell them?

Journal

See page 58, part 2 of your journal.

Prayer

If you have pictures or mementos of loved ones who have died, set them on the prayer table. Spend some time telling stories about them. Then pray:

In spirit, let us join in prayer
with the angels, our relatives, friends,
and all of the saints.
O God of the living,
we thank you for the gift
of life everlasting.
We shall live forever
with you and those whom we love.
We thank you in Jesus' name. Amen.

Blessing

Bless each other, and say:

(Name), God loves you with an everlasting love.
In the name of the Father, and of the Son,
and of the Holy Spirit. Amen.

Thirty-third Sunday in Ordinary Time

I Am with You Always

Based on Luke 21:5–19

Opening Question

Talk about some recent natural disasters. How do people cope or continue to have hope after a crisis?

Story

Read or reread "Cheering Up Aunt Liz," a story of hope in God, found on page 2 of this book.

Talk About the Story

Tell about a time when you or someone you know felt like Aunt Liz. What did you do?

Journal

See page 59, part 1 of your journal.

Scripture

God is in the picture even during gloomy and disastrous times. Read Luke 21:5–19 to see how God stays with us no matter what happens.

> A reading from the holy gospel according to Luke
>
> Some people were talking about the beautiful stones used to build the temple and about the gifts that had been placed in it.
>
> Jesus said, "Do you see these stones? The time is coming when not one of them will be left in place. They will be knocked down."
>
> Some people asked, "Teacher, when will all this happen? How can we know when these things are about to take place?"
>
> Jesus replied: "Don't be fooled by all those men who will come and claim to be me. They will say, 'I am Christ!' and 'Now is the time!' But don't follow them. When you hear about wars and riots, don't be afraid. These things will have to happen first, but that is not the end. "Nations will go to war against one another, and kingdoms will attack each other. There will be great earthquakes, and in many places people will starve to death and suffer terrible diseases. All sorts of frightening things will be seen in the sky.
>
> "Before all this happens, you will be arrested and punished. You will be tried in the Jewish meeting places and put in jail. Because of me you will be placed on trial before kings and governors. But this will be your chance to tell about your faith.
>
> "Don't worry about what you will say to defend yourselves. I will give you the wisdom to know what to say. None of your enemies will be able to oppose you or to say that you are wrong.

"You will be betrayed by your own parents, brothers, family, and friends. Some of you will even be killed. Because of me you will be hated by everyone. But don't worry! You will be saved by being faithful to me."

The gospel of the Lord.

Reflection

What is Jesus telling us in this scripture? What might give you hope when you suffer?

Journal

See page 59, part 2 of your journal.

Prayer

God, our constant hope,
we thank you for always being with us.
Help us to remember this
when we are frightened or hurting.
We ask this in Jesus' name. Amen.

Blessing

With a hug, assure your child that you want to help when life becomes difficult. Then bless each other with the following prayer:

(Name), God is with you in good times and in bad. Always remember that you are blessed. In the name of the Father, and of the Son, and of the Holy Spirit. Amen.

Thirty-fourth Sunday in Ordinary Time

Christ the King

Based on Luke 23:35 – 43

Opening Question

Imagine you are a king or a queen. What privileges would you want? What powers would you insist on having? What rules would you make for the people to obey?

Journal

See page 60, part 1 of your journal.

Scripture

Jesus is the king of kings. He is not like earthly kings. Read Luke 23:35 – 43 to discover what kind of king Jesus is.

> A reading from the holy gospel according to Luke
>
> While the crowd stood there watching Jesus, the leaders insulted him by saying, "He saved others. Now he should save himself, if he really is God's chosen Messiah!"
>
> The soldiers made fun of Jesus and brought him some wine. They said, "If you are the king of the Jews, save yourself!" Above him was a sign that said, "This is the King of the Jews."
>
> One of the criminals hanging there also insulted Jesus by saying, "Aren't you the Messiah? Save yourself and save us!"
>
> But the other criminal told the first one off, "Don't you fear God? Aren't you getting the same punishment as this man? We got what was coming to us, but he didn't do anything wrong." Then he said to Jesus, "Remember me when you come into power!"
>
> Jesus replied, "I promise that today you will be with me in paradise."
>
> The gospel of the Lord.

Reflection

What would it have been like if you were in the crowd watching the crucifixion? How would you have felt?

Journal

See page 60, part 2 of your journal.

Prayer

Parent, place a crucifix on the prayer table, and pray:

Jesus, king of heaven and earth,
you are like no other king or queen.
You gave your life on the cross
that we might live forever.
You gave us this world
but are always here with us.
You love us and forgive us.
May you reign as king forever and ever. Amen.

Blessing

While holding the crucifix, make a cross over each other, saying:

(Name), may Jesus, our king, reign in your heart always.
In the name of the Father, and of the Son, and of the Holy Spirit. Amen.

Guide for the Faith Formation Director

Listening to God's Word is a supplemental tool for parents or guardians who are preparing children for the sacraments of initiation: baptism, confirmation and eucharist. It consists of several parts: a book containing the gospel stories for every Sunday of the year (from the Contemporary English Version of the Bible, which is the translation used in the *Lectionary for Masses with Children*), with illustrative stories about the message of the gospels, games, activities, prayers, blessings and questions for reflection; a journal for the child; and an adult's journal. Eventually the series will have books and journals for Years A, B and C, and for the period of the precatechumenate for any time of the year.

Listening to God's Word is not intended to replace the faith formation process based in the life of the parish community. Rather, it offers an opportunity for parents and children, in their own homes, to spend time together with the scriptures that are proclaimed at the Sunday liturgy, to reflect on those scriptures and to pray together. The suggestions in these books help establish and strengthen the habits of communication and family prayer in the home. They enrich and are enriched by the gatherings for scriptural reflection, catechetical formation, prayer and apostolic service that constitute the Christian initiation process.

Though this book is intended for use by families at home, you may wish to use one or more of the sessions at gatherings of catechumens' families, particularly early in the period of the catechumenate. Modeling a session or two in the larger group may help parents feel more confident in initiating sessions with their children at home. Periodically throughout the catechumenate, such a session may help families become comfortable sharing faith and prayer with larger groups.

This supplement offers suggestions for a special moment during the period of the catechumenate: preparation for the rite of election. It follows the same format as the home sessions in the rest of this book, so it should be a comfortable format for those who have been using this book throughout the catechumenate. All the directions in this session are addressed to the catechist.

Preparing for the Rite of Election

Welcome

Opening Question

Tell a short story about a time when you were chosen to do something, such as being called to be a catechist, being chosen in marriage or being elected a club president. Then ask the group: Can you remember a time when you were chosen or elected to do something special? How did you feel when you were chosen? Share your stories with your family.

Story

Today's story is about someone who was chosen.

A New Captain

"Hey, runt, I'll never pick you for my team," Allen yelled. As he did, he imitated Roger, running with short steps from first to second base. Buzz and Toad squatted down to Roger's level and followed Allen and Roger around the bases to home plate.

"Roger's a turtle! Roger's a turtle!" they chanted. Roger didn't answer. His face crimson, his jaws clenched, he grabbed his bat and ball and ran into the brick school building. He threw the equipment into the musty-smelling sports closet and headed for home.

The next morning, Roger stood against his bedroom door eyeing the marks reflected in his wardrobe mirror. Every year his father would ink his growth on the pine door, and every morning Roger would hope that magically he had grown during the night. No change since yesterday or the week before that or the month before that. He pounded his fist on the door as if that would make the mark rise another inch.

Roger forced himself to ignore the aroma of gingerbread still in the oven. "I have to get to school early to practice," he called to his mother as he ran through the kitchen.

"Roger, come back here," his mother scolded, "You haven't even touched your breakfast." Roger was already out the door and down the street. "That boy," she sighed as she turned to the cat and poured Roger's milk into Mootsie's bowl. "All he ever thinks of is baseball."

"Mee-ow," Mootsie agreed, lapping the milk greedily.

Darla was waiting for Roger at the corner. "We can practice almost an hour before school starts," she said excitedly, her red braids dancing and glistening in the sun as the two raced the three blocks to Harlow School.

The baseball diamond was deserted. "Good," Roger thought with relief. Allen's voice calling him a runt and a turtle still grated in his ears like fingernails scraping a chalkboard. The two began pitching and hitting furiously. Crack! Crack! Crack! Again and again the ball soared high in the sky. Roger's father had told him once that hitting a baseball took more skill than any other sport. "You're using a curved bat to hit a curved ball," he had said, "and that's hard." Yet Darla hit as though she were born to it.

"I'd pick her if I were chosen captain," he thought, but he knew that being elected was just a dream. Allen had been captain last year, though no one really liked him. Everyone guessed that he'd be chosen again. Roger couldn't figure it out. Allen was already bossing and bullying the players around as though he ran the team.

Neither Darla nor Roger had noticed Mr. Watson, the new teacher, and a group of students standing behind them watching them practice. The buzzer for class sounded.

"You two are very good ball players," Mr. Watson acknowledged as the class scuffled into the red brick building.

"We practice every day," Darla replied.

Allen brushed past. "No runts or turtles on my team," he whispered into Roger's ear so Mr. Watson wouldn't hear him. Roger ignored him.

When the recess bell rang, Mr. Watson waved for everyone to remain in their seats. "As you know, class, today we will elect our new baseball captain." When Mr. Watson turned his back to pick up a piece of chalk, Allen stood up, bowed and rumpled Roger's hair.

"Cut that out," Roger commanded. Buzz and Toad snickered until Mr. Watson silenced them all with one of his looks.

"This year when you vote, I want you to consider more than who is the best catcher or who was captain last year," Mr. Watson went on. Allen shifted in his seat uncomfortably. He had nothing to say for once.

"If you wanted help with your pitching or fielding, who would you ask for help? I won't be out there all the time while you're practicing. The captain is your leader. A good captain will choose those who can play their positions well, not just choose friends."

Roger thought of Allen. "If I were captain, I'd have to pick him because he is a good player, but I'd put him in the outfield where he could yell around and talk to everybody. He doesn't have enough concentration for first base." Roger caught himself. He sighed. "But they're not going to elect me." Yet he knew he would make a good captain. He would care about his team and help them whenever they asked. The tick-tock of the clock on the wall was like a drumbeat in the quiet room. Roger would never forget what happened next, because it changed his whole life.

"Class, I'd like to say one more thing before you vote." Mr. Watson wrote three names on the chalkboard: Ralph Kiner, Willie Keeler and Roy Campanella. "What do these three men have in common?" he asked.

"Anybody knows that," Allen scoffed. "They're all baseball players."

"Allen knows his baseball history," Roger admitted to himself.

"What else?" Mr. Watson prodded.

"They're all in the Baseball Hall of Fame," Roger guessed, thinking of the baseball cards he had begun saving in first grade.

"You're right. But there's something else."

No one knew.

"Willie Keeler was called Wee Willie because he was less than five and a half feet tall."

"Wee Roger," Allen whispered. Roger clenched his fists. Wouldn't this guy ever let up?

"But," Mr. Watson looked right at Roger, "Willie was the greatest place hitter in baseball. Roy Campanella was chubby, but he was an outstanding catcher for the Brooklyn Dodgers. Ralph Kiner was a slow runner, and he still made it to baseball's Hall of Fame. So you see, all three men had something that could handicap them as baseball players, but they didn't let that stop them. Now, class, think hard and vote."

After a few minutes, Mr. Watson broke the silence. "Buzz, please collect the ballots. Allen, please tally the results on the chalkboard." Mr. Watson picked up a ballot and opened it. "Allen," he read. By the time the fourth ballot was read, Allen was smiling. He already had three marks next to his name. Then things began to change. Roger heard his name called three times in a row. He felt excited. But when his name was called for the eighth time and the election was over, he couldn't believe it.

"Final count is Roger, 8; Allen, 5; Buzz, 3; Darla, 4; Mindy, 1; and Don, 2," Mr. Watson announced.

Within seconds, Roger was in the middle of a swarm of classmates.

"Can I be pitcher?"

"Can I be catcher?"

"Can I play first base?"

Suddenly Roger was the most popular person in the room. He felt good. He forgot about Allen and his nasty remarks about his height. It was he, not Allen, who had been chosen by his classmates, something he had never expected. His thoughts soared until a voice broke in — a voice he had come to dread.

"Can I be pitcher?" Allen whined.

At that moment Roger knew that he would never again be afraid of that voice. He answered confidently, "That depends on the tryouts. I'll see."

Talk About the Story

Invite the adults and children to respond to the following questions.

If you were one of the people in this story, what would you have seen? What would you have heard? What would you have felt?

Scripture

Jesus wanted helpers who would make good leaders. Let's read Mark 1:14–20 to see how Jesus began his mission.

A reading from the holy gospel according to Mark

After John was arrested, Jesus went to Galilee and told the good news that comes from God. He said, "The time has come! God's kingdom will soon be here. Turn back to God and believe the good news!"

As Jesus was walking along the shore of Lake Galilee, he saw Simon and his brother Andrew. They were fishermen and were casting their nets into the lake. Jesus said to them, "Come with me! I will teach you how to bring in people instead of fish." Right then the two brothers dropped their nets and went with him.

Jesus walked on and soon saw James and John, the sons of Zebedee. They were in a boat, mending their nets. At once Jesus asked them to come with him. They left their father in the boat with the hired workers and went with him.

The gospel of the Lord.

Reflection

Ask the adults and children to think about the following question. Invite them to write their answers on a sheet of paper or draw a series of pictures with captions under each one (have art supplies ready). During the refreshment break, post the pictures on a wall for the group to enjoy. Imagine that you were in the boat and Jesus was talking to you. What would it have been like to be chosen by Jesus?

Refreshments

Prayer and Blessings

Adapt this prayer and blessing to fit the people and the circumstances, particularly if the children to be elected will be taking part in the parish's rite of sending.

Invite the children to form a circle around the prayer table. Families and sponsors should stand behind the children. Then begin with the following or something similar:

Let's close our eyes and be aware that God is right here with us. *(Pause.)*

Dear God,
thank you for choosing all of us to be your friends.
We thank you for the gift of each person here,
and we ask your blessing
that we may do the work you have given us.
Bless the parents, that they may be good models
of how to live the gospel.
Bless the sponsors, that they may continue to support
the elect and their families with friendship and prayer.
Bless the catechists, that they may continue
to lead and encourage us and others in the faith.
Bless the children, whom you have chosen
to receive baptism, confirmation and eucharist.
We now send them to our Bishop *(Name)*,
for they are ready for their final preparation
for the Easter sacraments.
In the name of the Father, and of the Son,
and of the Holy Spirit. Amen.

Let us return to our homes in the peace of Christ.
Thanks be to God.

SUPPLEMENT

Activities for Advent & Christmas

You may wish to choose one or more of the following activities this week. Whatever you do, have fun with each other.

1. Make a nativity set out of paper, clay or play dough. You might want to make play dough ahead of time.

   > *A Handy Recipe*
   >
   > Combine in a saucepan:
   > 1 cup flour
   > ½ cup salt
   > 2 teaspoons cream of tartar
   > 1 cup water
   > 1 tablespoon oil
   >
   > Cook over medium heat. Stir constantly until mixture forms a ball. Cool. Store in an airtight container. You may wish to make several batches and add food coloring for the different pieces in the set.

2. Some parishes collect gifts for poor families. Together, buy and wrap gifts for this parish project.

3. Bake and decorate cookies, and give some as a gift.

4. At Christmas Mass, visit the manger in the church.

5. Take a walking tour around your neighborhood, or drive around town looking for outdoor Nativity sets.

6. Read and enjoy the Christmas play found at the end of this list.

7. Make a large nativity or holiday banner for inside or outside your home. Use bright, festive colors and materials that are heavy. (Such as felt, upholstery fabric or material for sailboats that would be durable for outdoors.)

8. Make a nativity movie out of white shelf paper, a cardboard box and two dowels several inches wider than the box. Cut a "window" the height and width of the shelf paper in the cardboard box so that it looks like a television.

   Next, cut holes on both sides of the box (top and bottom) so that the dowels can be turned and advance the movie pictures. See the illustration below. Then with a pencil, divide the shelf paper into equal spaces to fit the size of the "window." Allow the first space to be blank and the second for the title and credits.

   After reading the Christmas story together or the play in this book, decide what pictures you and your child would like to draw for the movie. When the pictures are complete, securely attach both ends of the shelf paper to the dowels. Turn the movie so that the paper is firmly around the bottom dowel, allowing the title page to be seen in the "window."

   Your child may enjoy presenting the movie to Christmas guests.

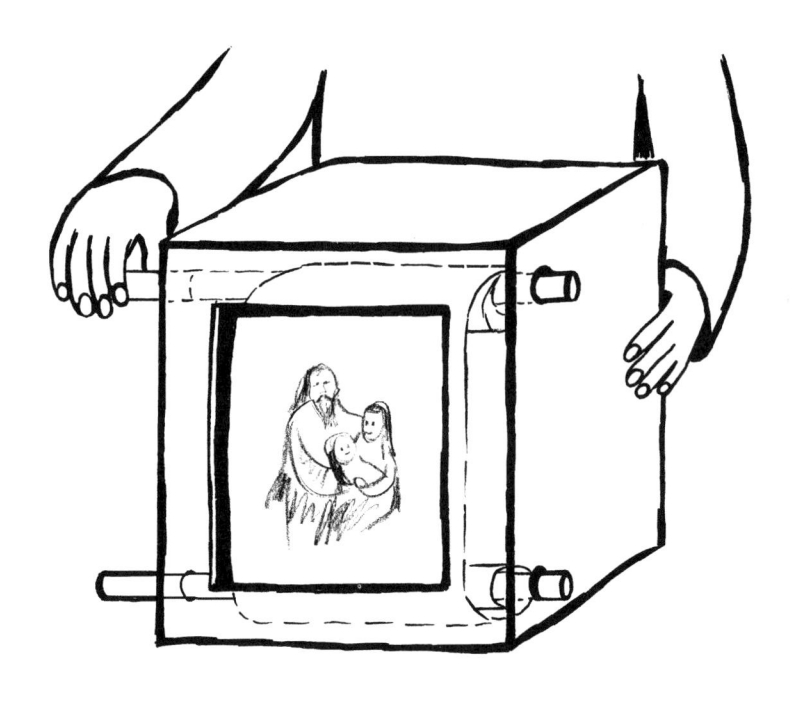

A Christmas Play

In this play you will read about God asking a woman named Mary for a very special favor. It is adapted from Luke 1:26–38. If your family is small, you will each need to take more than one part. There are nine characters: Mary, Anne, Joachim, the angel Gabriel, Elizabeth, Joseph the innkeeper, two shepherds and the narrator.

Scene 1

Narrator	What you are about to hear is a story of faith. It is a story about God's marvelous love for us. God sent us a gift above all other gifts. Come back in time with me. We'll travel 2,000 years back in time to the village of Nazareth. We listen to a young woman, Mary, talking with her mother, Anne.
Mary	Mother, Joseph has asked me to marry him, and I want to so much.
Anna	Your father and I have talked about it, Mary. He likes Joseph.
Narrator	Mary's father, Joachim, comes in and joins the conversation.
Joachim	My little Mary, it seems so strange that you're all grown up and old enough to have a husband. Joseph is a good man. There is no one else I would want you to marry.
Mary	Oh! I'm so happy!
Narrator	So Mary and Joseph were engaged. End of scene 1.

Scene 2

Narrator	Before Mary and Joseph got married, God sent a messenger to Mary. Scene 2 begins with Mary and the angel Gabriel. Mary is alone in the house. She sees a shadow and thinks that her mother has come back from getting water at the well.
Mary	Mother, are you back already?
Angel	Hello, Mary. God has looked on you with kindness and given you a great blessing.
Narrator	Mary is startled by the stranger and surprised by what he says.

152   Activities Advent & Christmas

Mary	What? Who are you?
Angel	I am the angel Gabriel. God sent me to tell you that you are blessed.
Mary	Me? I'm just a young girl. What do you mean?
Angel	You are going to have a son, and you will name him Jesus. He will be a man of great honor, and he will be called Son of the Most High.
Mary	How can this happen? Joseph and I aren't even married yet.
Angel	God's Spirit will come over you. Your child will be the Son of God. There is nothing impossible with God. God can do all things.
Narrator	Mary listened with her heart to what the angel said. Then she bowed to him and said:
Mary	I will do whatever God wants.
Narrator	End of Scene Two. The next scene opens with Mary visiting her cousin Elizabeth. Elizabeth needs help because she too is expecting a baby.

Scene 3

Mary	*(Knocks on Elizabeth's door)* Elizabeth, are you home?
Elizabeth	Mary, what a wonderful surprise! Blessed are you among all women. Blessed is the child within you! Who am I that the mother of God's Son should come to visit me? The moment I heard you, my own baby stirred in my womb for joy. Blessed are you to have such faith in God.
Narrator	The two grace-filled women talked and enjoyed each other's company for three months while they waited for Elizabeth's baby to arrive. Elizabeth's baby was named John. He grew up to be John the Baptist. Mary then returned home, and Joseph realized that Mary was pregnant. He knew that the baby was not his child. Joseph worried about this and wondered if he should continue with the wedding plans. Joseph prayed and brought his worry before the Lord. God answered his prayer with a message. As Scene 4 opens, Joseph is dreaming about his problem.

Scene 4

Angel	*(An angel comes into the room and stands next to Joseph.)* Joseph, take Mary as your wife. The Holy Spirit has come over her. She will have God's Son, and you will call him Jesus.
Joseph	*(Wakes up and talks to himself)* An angel has come to me in a dream. I must go to Mary and arrange the marriage. I trust that God will care for us.
Narrator	Mary and Joseph were married. They were both happy as they prepared for Jesus' birth. Then news came that would cause great hardship for them. Scene 5 opens with a typical day in Nazareth.

Scene 5

Mary	*(Mary sweeps the floor as Joseph comes into the house. She looks up.)* Hello, Joseph. You look worried.
Joseph	Mary, I've got some bad news. The Emperor, Caesar Augustus, wants a census to find out how many people are in his kingdom. We must go to Bethlehem and be counted. This will be a hard trip for you, Mary. Jesus will be born soon.
Mary	Joseph, don't worry. Let's get ready to go.

Activities for Advent & Christmas

Narrator	The trip was long and hard. Scene 6 opens with Mary and Joseph in Bethlehem; Joseph is knocking on the door to an inn.

Scene 6

Innkeeper	*(Opens door)* Yes? What can I do for you?
Joseph	My wife is expecting to give birth soon. We need a quiet place to stay. Every inn is filled.
Innkeeper	I have no room in the house. Would you like to use the stable out in the back? The animals will keep it warm for you.
Joseph	Yes. Thank you.
Narrator	Well, God's greatest gift was born in a stable. Scene 7 begins with a spectacular announcement. Some shepherds were tending their flocks that night, and suddenly they saw a bright light in the sky.

Scene 7

Shepherd 1	*(Surprised)* Oh-h-h look at that light!
Shepherd 2	*(Fearful)* What is it?
Angel	You have nothing to fear. I come to give you great news. Today, in Bethlehem, a savior has been born. He is the Messiah, the one for whom you have been waiting. Let this be a sign. In a manger, you will find an infant wrapped in swaddling clothes.
Shepherd 2	Come, let's go to Bethlehem and see this marvelous sight.
Angels	*(Everybody)* Glory to God in high heaven. Peace on earth to those whom God favors.
Narrator	When the shepherds arrived at the stable, the felt shy about going in. They knocked quietly on the door.
Joseph	*(Opens the door and smiles at the shepherds)* Please come in and see little Jesus.
Shepherd 2	*(Enters and kneels before the baby)* Thank you, God, for sending us the savior of the world.
Narrator	Yes, thank you, God, for your greatest gift, Jesus, the savior of the world.
All Sing	O come, all ye faithful, joyful and triumphant, O come ye, O come ye, to Bethlehem; Come and behold him, Born the King of angels; O come, let us adore him, O come, let us adore him, O come, let us adore him, Christ, the Lord!

Stand Up Game

Cut apart the cards below and stack them face down. Each player draws a card. Think about a Christian solution to the problem presented. When ready, stand up and share what you would like to do in the particular situation. When all of the cards have been drawn, place them on the prayer table.

If you want more "Stand Up" situations, fill in the cards below.

When everyone is laughing at another's mistake, I would like to _____ .	When I see a friend bullying another, I would like to _____ .
When I see a street person, I would like to _____ .	When someone teases a dog, I would like to _____ .
When someone looks or acts differently from my family, I would like to _____ .	If I had a million dollars, I would like to _____ .
When someone starts a fight, I would like to _____ .	If someone ridicules another's religious beliefs, I would like to _____ .
When I hear about war, I would like to _____ .	When a neighbor is sick, I would like to _____ .
When I read about people who are starving, I would like to _____ .	When a friend's parent is in jail, I would like to _____ .

Stand Up Game   155

Discovery Game

This game can be played with two or more players. Cut apart the cards below. Stack the cards in a pile, face down. Each person draws a card. Finish the sentence by describing the person on your left. If the person on the left disagrees with the answer, she or he is allowed to give hints. For example: Player 1 says: "Your favorite color is pink." The person on the left could say: "No, my favorite color is a fruit that I ate for breakfast." Place completed cards on the bottom of the stack, and each player draws again. For new ideas, make up your own cards with the blanks below.

Your favorite ice cream flavor is _____ .	Your favorite song is _____ .
For the next family vacation, you want to go _____ .	You like to _____ for relaxation.
On your days off from work or school, you like to _____ .	Your favorite animal is a _____ .
What you like about me most is _____ .	Your favorite thing to do is _____ .
Your least favorite task is _____ .	One of the stories that you enjoy is _____ .

Who Are My Neighbors? Game

Cut the following cards apart and place them in a pile, face down.

MARKERS: Use different colored buttons, noodles, spools of thread or anything in the house that would make a marker for each player. Place markers at START on the game board.

TO BEGIN: Write numbers on small pieces of paper, fold and put in a deep bowl. Each player draws a number. #1 starts, then #2, etc. by picking up the top card from the pile. Answer the question and move the appropriate marker according to the directions. Then place the completed card under the pile.

BE CREATIVE: Write some of your own situations with the blank cards provided.

Tim gave Sally some tissue when she sniffled in class. **Move forward two spaces.**	Sam invited a classmate who didn't have many friends to eat lunch with him. **Move forward 5 spaces.**
Bill helped an elderly person safely cross the street. **Move forward 2 spaces.**	John teased Ralph because he wore glasses. **Move back 4 spaces.**
Larry took lemonade to the thirsty field workers. **Move forward 4 spaces.**	Shane helped Ryan with math problems. **Move forward 3 spaces.**
Maria apologized after saying unkind things to Alice. **Move forward 4 spaces.**	Some girls talked unkindly about Judy behind her back. **Move back 4 spaces.**
Ryan laughed when Shane made a mistake. **Move back 3 spaces.**	Bill refused to let anyone touch his football. **Move back 3 spaces.**
Liz smiled and held the door for Vicki, who was in a wheelchair. **Move forward 3 spaces.**	Taylor was too busy to give his dog fresh water for the day. **Move back 4 spaces.**
Kyle started a campaign to collect food for the hungry. **Move forward 5 spaces.**	Jack ignored his brother when he asked for help with his homework. **Move back 3 spaces.**
Tina had a jacket and sweater and let Elsie, who was cold, wear one. **Move forward 4 spaces.**	Mom scolded before she heard Mary's story about being late. **Move back 3 spaces.**
Ted didn't share his candy with a companion. **Move back 3 spaces.**	Sue washed her little sister's dirty hands before supper. **Move forward 4 spaces.**

"No!" said Kris when a classmate pushed marijuana at her. **Move forward 5 spaces.**	Dad helped Adam with his Reading workbook. **Move forward 3 spaces.**
Jane visited her friend who couldn't go to school because she had broken her leg. **Move forward 4 spaces.**	Ned offered Jim some beer after his dad left the house. **Move back 5 spaces.**
A parent works hard to keep a roof over the family. **Move forward 5 spaces.**	Jerry was very good at baseball. Sometimes he'd practice with those who needed help. **Move forward 4 spaces.**
Eileen reads stories to her younger sisters. **Move forward 4 spaces.**	Mom feeds the family. **Move forward 5 spaces.**
Joan is patient when her little brother doesn't understand something. **Move forward 4 spaces.**	Ray plans special things to do when he babysits. **Move forward 4 spaces.**
The teacher refused to let the pupils laugh at others' mistakes. **Move forward 4 spaces.**	Steve always shoves and wants to be first. **Move back 4 spaces.**

Who Are My Neighbors? Game 161

Who Are My Neighbors?

START

GOOD NEIGHBOR

```
  409
× 396
―――――
 2454
 3681
1227
```

I Believe Game

Cut apart the cards. Stack them upside down. Take turns pulling a card and telling what you believe about the word printed on the card. You may want to make up some of your own cards.

Family	Jesus
Nature	God
Forgiveness	Love
Friendship	Eucharist
Life	Death
Church	Gift-giving
Easter	Heaven
Keeping my word	Honesty

Calendar

Sunday/Feast Day	1998	1999	2000
	Year C	Year A	Year B
1st Sunday of Advent	November 30, 1997	November 29, 1998	November 28, 1999
2nd Sunday of Advent	December 7, 1997	December 6, 1998	December 5, 1999
3rd Sunday of Advent	December 14, 1997	December 13, 1998	December 12, 1999
4th Sunday of Advent	December 21, 1997	December 20, 1998	December 19, 1999
Christmas, December 25	Thursday	Friday	Saturday
Holy Family	December 28, 1997	December 27, 1998	December 26, 2000
Epiphany	January 4, 1998	January 3, 1999	January 2, 2000
Baptism of the Lord	January 11, 1998	January 10, 1999	January 9, 2000
2nd Sunday in Ordinary Time	January 18	January 17	January 16
3rd Sunday in Ordinary Time	January 25	January 24	January 23
4th Sunday in Ordinary Time	February 1	January 31	January 30
5th Sunday in Ordinary Time	February 8	February 7	February 6
6th Sunday in Ordinary Time	February 15	February 14	February 13
7th Sunday in Ordinary Time	February 22	—	February 20
8th Sunday in Ordinary Time	—	—	February 27
9th Sunday in Ordinary Time	—	—	March 5
Ash Wednesday	February 25	February 17	March 8
1st Sunday of Lent	March 1	February 21	March 12
2nd Sunday of Lent	March 8	February 28	March 19
3rd Sunday of Lent	March 15	March 7	March 26
4th Sunday of Lent	March 22	March 14	April 2
5th Sunday of Lent	March 29	March 21	April 9
Passion (Palm) Sunday	April 5	March 28	April 16
Holy Thursday	April 9	April 1	April 20
Good Friday	April 10	April 2	April 21
Easter Sunday	April 12	April 4	April 23
2nd Sunday of Easter	April 19	April 11	April 30
3rd Sunday of Easter	April 26	April 18	May 7
4th Sunday of Easter	May 3	April 25	May 14
5th Sunday of Easter	May 10	May 2	May 21
6th Sunday of Easter	May 17	May 9	May 28
Ascension	May 21	May 13	June 1
7th Sunday of Easter	May 24	May 16	June 4
Pentecost	May 31	May 23	June 11
Trinity Sunday	June 7	May 30	June 18
Body and Blood of Christ	June 14	June 6	June 25
9th Sunday in Ordinary Time	—	—	—
10th Sunday in Ordinary Time	—	—	—
11th Sunday in Ordinary Time	—	June 13	—
12th Sunday in Ordinary Time	June 21	June 20	—
13th Sunday in Ordinary Time	June 28	June 27	July 2
14th Sunday in Ordinary Time	July 5	July 4	July 9
15th Sunday in Ordinary Time	July 12	July 11	July 16
16th Sunday in Ordinary Time	July 19	July 18	July 23

Sunday/Feast Day	1998 (cont.)	1999 (cont.)	2000 (cont.)
	Year C	Year A	Year B
17th Sunday in Ordinary Time	July 26	July 25	July 30
18th Sunday in Ordinary Time	August 2	August 1	—[3]
19th Sunday in Ordinary Time	August 9	August 8	August 13
20th Sunday in Ordinary Time	August 16	—[2]	August 20
21st Sunday in Ordinary Time	August 23	August 22	August 27
22nd Sunday in Ordinary Time	August 30	August 29	September 3
23rd Sunday in Ordinary Time	September 6	September 5	September 10
24th Sunday in Ordinary Time	September 13	September 12	September 17
25th Sunday in Ordinary Time	September 20	September 19	September 24
26th Sunday in Ordinary Time	September 27	September 26	October 1
27th Sunday in Ordinary Time	October 4	October 3	Octobber 8
28th Sunday in Ordinary Time	October 11	October 10	October 15
29th Sunday in Ordinary Time	October 18	October 17	October 22
30th Sunday in Ordinary Time	October 25	October 24	October 29
31st Sunday in Ordinary Time	—[1]	October 31	November 5
32nd Sunday in Ordinary Time	November 8	November 7	November 12
33rd Sunday in Ordinary Time	November 15	November 14	November 19
Christ the King	November 22	November 21	November 26

Sunday/Feast Day	2001	2002	2003
	Year C	Year A	Year B
1st Sunday of Advent	December 3, 2000	December 2, 2001	December 1, 2002
2nd Sunday of Advent	December 10, 2000	December 9, 2001	December 8, 2002
3rd Sunday of Advent	December 17, 2000	December 16, 2001	December 15, 2002
4th Sunday of Advent	December 24, 2000	December 23, 2001	December 22, 2002
Christmas, December 25	Monday	Tuesday	Wednesday
Holy Family	December 31, 2000	December 30, 2001	December 29, 2002
Epiphany	January 7, 2001	January 6, 2002	January 5, 2003
Baptism of the Lord	January 8, 2001†	January 13, 2002	January 12, 2003
2nd Sunday in Ordinary Time	January 14	January 20	January 19
3rd Sunday in Ordinary Time	January 21	January 27	January 26
4th Sunday in Ordinary Time	January 28	February 3	—[4]
5th Sunday in Ordinary Time	February 4	February 10	February 9
6th Sunday in Ordinary Time	February 11	—	February 16
7th Sunday in Ordinary Time	February 18	—	February 23
8th Sunday in Ordinary Time	February 25	—	March 2
9th Sunday in Ordinary Time	—	—	—
Ash Wednesday	February 28	February 13	March 5
1st Sunday of Lent	March 4	February 17	March 9
2nd Sunday of Lent	March 11	February 24	March 16

† This feast is celebrated this year on a weekday.
1. The celebration of this Sunday is superceded by the feast of All Saints.
2. The celebration of this Sunday is superceded by the Assumption.
3. The celebration of this Sunday is superceded by the Transfiguration.
4. The celebration of this Sunday is superceded by the Presentation of the Lord.

Sunday/Feast Day	2001 (cont.)	2002 (cont.)	2003 (cont.)
	Year C	Year A	Year B
3rd Sunday of Lent	March 18	March 3	March 23
4th Sunday of Lent	March 25	March 10	March 30
5th Sunday of Lent	April 1	March 17	April 6
Passion (Palm) Sunday	April 8	March 24	April 13
Holy Thursday	April 12	March 28	April 17
Good Friday	April 13	March 29	April 18
Easter Sunday	April 15	March 31	April 20
2nd Sunday of Easter	April 22	April 7	April 27
3rd Sunday of Easter	April 29	April 14	May 4
4th Sunday of Easter	May 6	April 21	May 11
5th Sunday of Easter	May 13	April 28	May 18
6th Sunday of Easter	May 20	May 5	May 25
Ascension	May 24	May 9	May 29
7th Sunday of Easter	May 27	May 12	June 1
Pentecost	June 3	May 19	June 8
Trinity Sunday	June 10	May 26	June 15
Body and Blood of Christ	June 17	June 2	June 22
9th Sunday in Ordinary Time	—	—	—
10th Sunday in Ordinary Time	—	June 9	—
11th Sunday in Ordinary Time	—	June 16	—
12th Sunday in Ordinary Time	—[5]	June 23	—
13th Sunday in Ordinary Time	July 1	June 30	—[6]
14th Sunday in Ordinary Time	July 8	July 7	July 6
15th Sunday in Ordinary Time	July 15	July 14	July 13
16th Sunday in Ordinary Time	July 22	July 21	July 20
17th Sunday in Ordinary Time	July 29	July 28	July 27
18th Sunday in Ordinary Time	August 5	August 4	August 3
19th Sunday in Ordinary Time	August 12	August 11	August 10
20th Sunday in Ordinary Time	August 19	August 18	August 17
21st Sunday in Ordinary Time	August 26	August 25	August 24
22nd Sunday in Ordinary Time	September 2	September 1	August 31
23rd Sunday in Ordinary Time	September 9	September 8	September 7
24th Sunday in Ordinary Time	September 16	September 15	—[7]
25th Sunday in Ordinary Time	September 23	September 22	September 21
26th Sunday in Ordinary Time	September 30	September 29	September 28
27th Sunday in Ordinary Time	October 7	October 6	October 5
28th Sunday in Ordinary Time	October 14	October 13	October 12
29th Sunday in Ordinary Time	October 21	October 20	October 19
30th Sunday in Ordinary Time	October 28	October 27	October 26
31st Sunday in Ordinary Time	November 4	November 3	—[8]
32nd Sunday in Ordinary Time	November 11	November 10	—[9]
33rd Sunday in Ordinary Time	November 18	November 17	November 16
Christ the King	November 25	November 24	November 23

5. The celebration of this Sunday is superceded by the Birth of John the Baptist.
6. The celebration of this Sunday is superceded by the feast of Peter and Paul, Apostles.
7. The celebration of this Sunday is superceded by the feast of the Triumph of the Cross.
8. The celebration of this Sunday is superceded by the feast of All Souls.
9. The celebration of this Sunday is superceded by the feast of the Dedication of St. John Lateran.

Sunday/Feast Day	2004	2005	2006
	Year C	*Year A*	*Year B*
1st Sunday of Advent	November 30, 2003	November 28, 2004	November 27, 2005
2nd Sunday of Advent	December 7, 2003	December 5, 2004	December 4, 2005
3rd Sunday of Advent	December 14, 2003	December 12, 2004	December 11, 2005
4th Sunday of Advent	December 21, 2003	December 19, 2004	December 18, 2005
Christmas, December 25	Thursday	Saturday	Sunday
Holy Family	December 28, 2003	December 26, 2004	December 30, 2005†
Mary, Mother of God, January 1	Thursday	Saturday	Sunday
Epiphany	January 4, 2004	January 2, 2005	January 8, 2006
Baptism of the Lord	January 11, 2004	January 9, 2005	January 9, 2006†
2nd Sunday in Ordinary Time	January 18	January 16	January 15
3rd Sunday in Ordinary Time	January 25	January 23	January 22
4th Sunday in Ordinary Time	February 1	January 30	January 29
5th Sunday in Ordinary Time	February 8	February 6	February 5
6th Sunday in Ordinary Time	February 15	—	February 12
7th Sunday in Ordinary Time	February 22	—	February 19
8th Sunday in Ordinary Time	—	—	February 26
9th Sunday in Ordinary Time	—	—	—
Ash Wednesday	February 25	February 9	March 1
1st Sunday of Lent	February 29	February 13	March 5
2nd Sunday of Lent	March 7	February 20	March 12
3rd Sunday of Lent	March 14	February 27	March 19
4th Sunday of Lent	March 21	March 6	March 26
5th Sunday of Lent	March 28	March 13	April 2
Passion (Palm) Sunday	April 4	March 20	April 9
Holy Thursday	April 8	March 24	April 13
Good Friday	April 9	March 25	April 14
Easter Sunday	April 11	March 27	April 16
2nd Sunday of Easter	April 18	April 3	April 23
3rd Sunday of Easter	April 25	April 10	April 30
4th Sunday of Easter	May 2	April 17	May 7
5th Sunday of Easter	May 9	April 24	May 14
6th Sunday of Easter	May 16	May 1	May 21
Ascension	May 20	May 5	May 25
7th Sunday of Easter	May 23	May 8	May 28
Pentecost	May 30	May 15	June 4
Trinity Sunday	June 6	May 22	June 11
Body and Blood of Christ	June 13	May 29	June 18
9th Sunday in Ordinary Time	—	—	—
10th Sunday in Ordinary Time	—	June 5	—
11th Sunday in Ordinary Time	—	June 12	—
12th Sunday in Ordinary Time	June 20	June 19	June 25
13th Sunday in Ordinary Time	June 27	June 26	July 2
14th Sunday in Ordinary Time	July 4	July 3	July 9
15th Sunday in Ordinary Time	July 11	July 10	July 16

† This solemnity has been transferred to this date.

Sunday/Feast Day	2004 (cont.)	2005 (cont.)	2006 (cont.)
	Year C	Year A	Year B
16th Sunday in Ordinary Time	July 18	July 17	July 23
17th Sunday in Ordinary Time	July 25	July 24	July 30
18th Sunday in Ordinary Time	August 1	July 31	—[11]
19th Sunday in Ordinary Time	August 8	August 7	August 13
20th Sunday in Ordinary Time	—[10]	August 14	August 20
21st Sunday in Ordinary Time	August 22	August 21	August 27
22nd Sunday in Ordinary Time	August 29	August 28	September 3
23rd Sunday in Ordinary Time	September 5	September 4	September 10
24th Sunday in Ordinary Time	September 12	September 11	September 17
25th Sunday in Ordinary Time	September 19	September 18	September 24
26th Sunday in Ordinary Time	September 26	September 25	October 1
27th Sunday in Ordinary Time	October 3	October 2	October 8
28th Sunday in Ordinary Time	October 10	October 9	October 15
29th Sunday in Ordinary Time	October 17	October 16	October 22
30th Sunday in Ordinary Time	October 24	October 23	October 29
31st Sunday in Ordinary Time	October 31	October 30	November 5
32nd Sunday in Ordinary Time	November 7	November 6	November 12
33rd Sunday in Ordinary Time	November 14	November 13	November 19
Christ the King	November 21	November 20	November 26

Sunday/Feast Day	2007	2008	2009
	Year C	Year A	Year B
1st Sunday of Advent	December 3, 2006	December 2, 2007	November 30, 2008
2nd Sunday of Advent	December 10, 2006	December 9, 2007	December 7, 2008
3rd Sunday of Advent	December 17, 2006	December 16, 2007	December 14, 2008
4th Sunday of Advent	December 24, 2006	December 23, 2007	December 21, 2008
Christmas, December 25	Monday	Tuesday	Thursday
Holy Family	December 31, 2006	December 30, 2007	December 28, 2008
Epiphany	January 7, 2007	January 6, 2008	January 4, 2009
Baptism of the Lord	January 8, 2007†	January 13, 2008	January 11, 2009
2nd Sunday in Ordinary Time	January 14	January 20	January 18
3rd Sunday in Ordinary Time	January 21	January 27	January 25
4th Sunday in Ordinary Time	January 28	February 3	February 1
5th Sunday in Ordinary Time	February 4	—	February 8
6th Sunday in Ordinary Time	February 11	—	February 15
7th Sunday in Ordinary Time	February 18	—	February 22
8th Sunday in Ordinary Time	—	—	—
9th Sunday in Ordinary Time	—	—	—
Ash Wednesday	February 21	February 6	February 25
1st Sunday of Lent	February 25	February 10	March 1
2nd Sunday of Lent	March 4	February 17	March 8
3rd Sunday of Lent	March 11	February 24	March 15

† This solemnity has been transferred to this date.
10. The celebration of this Sunday is superceded by the feast of the Assumption.
11. The celebration of this Sunday is superceded by the feast of the Transfiguration.

Sunday/Feast Day	2007 *(cont.)*	2008 *(cont.)*	2009 *(cont.)*
	Year C	*Year A*	*Year B*
4th Sunday of Lent	March 18	March 2	March 22
5th Sunday of Lent	March 25	March 9	March 29
Passion (Palm) Sunday	April 1	March 16	April 5
Holy Thursday	April 5	March 20	April 9
Good Friday	April 6	March 21	April 10
Easter Sunday	April 8	March 23	April 12
2nd Sunday of Easter	April 15	March 30	April 19
3rd Sunday of Easter	April 22	April 6	April 26
4th Sunday of Easter	April 29	April 13	May 3
5th Sunday of Easter	May 6	April 20	May 10
6th Sunday of Easter	May 13	April 27	May 17
Ascension	May 17	May 1	May 21
7th Sunday of Easter	May 20	May 4	May 24
Pentecost	May 27	May 11	May 31
Trinity Sunday	June 3	May 18	June 7
Body and Blood of Christ	June 10	May 25	June 14
9th Sunday in Ordinary Time	—	June 1	—
10th Sunday in Ordinary Time	—	June 8	—
11th Sunday in Ordinary Time	June 17	June 15	—
12th Sunday in Ordinary Time	—[12]	June 22	June 21
13th Sunday in Ordinary Time	July 1	—[13]	June 28
14th Sunday in Ordinary Time	July 8	July 6	July 5
15th Sunday in Ordinary Time	July 15	July 13	July 12
16th Sunday in Ordinary Time	July 22	July 20	July 19
17th Sunday in Ordinary Time	July 29	July 27	July 26
18th Sunday in Ordinary Time	August 5	August 3	August 2
19th Sunday in Ordinary Time	August 12	August 10	August 9
20th Sunday in Ordinary Time	August 19	August 17	August 16
21st Sunday in Ordinary Time	August 26	August 24	August 23
22nd Sunday in Ordinary Time	September 2	August 31	August 30
23rd Sunday in Ordinary Time	September 9	September 7	September 6
24th Sunday in Ordinary Time	September 16	—[14]	September 13
25th Sunday in Ordinary Time	September 23	September 21	September 20
26th Sunday in Ordinary Time	September 30	September 28	September 27
27th Sunday in Ordinary Time	October 7	October 5	October 4
28th Sunday in Ordinary Time	October 14	October 12	October 11
29th Sunday in Ordinary Time	October 21	October 19	October 18
30th Sunday in Ordinary Time	October 28	October 26	October 25
31st Sunday in Ordinary Time	November 4	—[15]	—[17]
32nd Sunday in Ordinary Time	November 11	—[16]	November 8
33rd Sunday in Ordinary Time	November 18	November 16	November 15
Christ the King	November 25	November 23	November 22

12 The celebration of this Sunday is superceded by the Birth of John the Baptist.
13. The celebration of this Sunday is superceded by the feast of Peter and Paul, apostles.
14. The celebration of this Sunday is superceded by the Triumph of the Cross.
15. The celebration of this Sunday is superceded by the feast of All Souls.
16. The celebration of this Sunday is superceded by the Dedication of St. John Lateran.
17. The celebration of this Sunday is superceded by the feast of All Saints.

Sunday/Feast Day	2010	2011	2012
	Year C	Year A	Year B
1st Sunday of Advent	November 29, 2009	November 28, 2010	November 27, 2011
2nd Sunday of Advent	December 6, 2009	December 5, 2010	December 4, 2011
3rd Sunday of Advent	December 13, 2009	December 12, 2010	December 11, 2011
4th Sunday of Advent	December 20, 2009	December 19, 2010	December 18, 2011
Christmas, December 25	Friday	Saturday	Sunday
Holy Family	December 27, 2009	December 26, 2010	December 30, 2011†
Mary, Mother of God, January 1	Friday	Saturday	Sunday
Epiphany	January 3, 2010	January 2, 2011	January 8, 2012
Baptism of the Lord	January 10, 2010	January 9, 2011	January 9, 2012†
2nd Sunday in Ordinary Time	January 17	January 16	January 15
3rd Sunday in Ordinary Time	January 24	January 23	January 22
4th Sunday in Ordinary Time	January 31	January 30	January 29
5th Sunday in Ordinary Time	February 7	February 6	February 5
6th Sunday in Ordinary Time	February 14	February 13	February 12
7th Sunday in Ordinary Time	—	February 20	February 19
8th Sunday in Ordinary Time	—	February 27	—
9th Sunday in Ordinary Time	—	March 6	—
Ash Wednesday	February 17	March 9	February 22
1st Sunday of Lent	February 21	March 13	February 26
2nd Sunday of Lent	February 28	March 20	March 4
3rd Sunday of Lent	March 7	March 27	March 11
4th Sunday of Lent	March 14	April 3	March 18
5th Sunday of Lent	March 21	April 10	March 25
Passion (Palm) Sunday	March 28	April 17	April 1
Holy Thursday	April 1	April 21	April 5
Good Friday	April 2	April 22	April 6
Easter Sunday	April 4	April 24	April 8
2nd Sunday of Easter	April 11	May 1	April 15
3rd Sunday of Easter	April 18	May 8	April 22
4th Sunday of Easter	April 25	May 15	April 29
5th Sunday of Easter	May 2	May 22	May 6
6th Sunday of Easter	May 9	May 29	May 13
Ascension	May 13	June 2	May 17
7th Sunday of Easter	May 16	June 5	May 20
Pentecost	May 23	June 12	May 27
Trinity Sunday	May 30	June 19	June 3
Body and Blood of Christ	June 6	June 26	June 10
9th Sunday in Ordinary Time	—	—	—
10th Sunday in Ordinary Time	—	—	—
11th Sunday in Ordinary Time	June 13	—	June 17
12th Sunday in Ordinary Time	June 20	—	—[18]
13th Sunday in Ordinary Time	June 27	—	July 1
14th Sunday in Ordinary Time	July 4	July 3	July 8
15th Sunday in Ordinary Time	July 11	July 10	July 15

† This solemnity has been transferred to this date.
18. The celebration of this Sunday is superceded by the Birth of John the Baptist.

Sunday/Feast Day	2010 (cont.)	2011 (cont.)	2012 (cont.)
	Year C	Year A	Year B
16th Sunday in Ordinary Time	July 18	July 17	July 22
17th Sunday in Ordinary Time	July 25	July 24	July 29
18th Sunday in Ordinary Time	August 1	July 31	August 5
19th Sunday in Ordinary Time	August 8	August 7	August 12
20th Sunday in Ordinary Time	— [19]	August 14	August 19
21st Sunday in Ordinary Time	August 22	August 21	August 26
22nd Sunday in Ordinary Time	August 29	August 28	September 2
23rd Sunday in Ordinary Time	September 5	September 4	September 9
24th Sunday in Ordinary Time	September 12	September 11	September 16
25th Sunday in Ordinary Time	September 19	September 18	September 23
26th Sunday in Ordinary Time	September 26	September 25	September 30
27th Sunday in Ordinary Time	October 3	October 2	October 7
28th Sunday in Ordinary Time	October 10	October 9	October 14
29th Sunday in Ordinary Time	October 17	October 16	October 21
30th Sunday in Ordinary Time	October 24	October 23	October 28
31st Sunday in Ordinary Time	October 31	October 30	November 4
32nd Sunday in Ordinary Time	November 7	November 6	November 11
33rd Sunday in Ordinary Time	November 14	November 13	November 18
Christ the King	November 21	November 20	November 25

Sunday/Feast Day	2013	2014	2015
	Year C	Year A	Year B
1st Sunday of Advent	December 2, 2012	December 1, 2013	November 30, 2014
2nd Sunday of Advent	December 9, 2012	December 8, 2013	December 7, 2014
3rd Sunday of Advent	December 16, 2012	December 15, 2013	December 14, 2014
4th Sunday of Advent	December 23, 2012	December 22, 2013	December 21, 2014
Christmas, December 25	Tuesday	Wednesday	Thursday
Holy Family	December 30, 2012	December 29, 2013	December 28, 2014
Epiphany	January 6, 2013	January 5, 2014	January 4, 2015
Baptism of the Lord	January 13, 2013	January 12, 2014	January 11, 2015
2nd Sunday in Ordinary Time	January 20	January 19	January 18
3rd Sunday in Ordinary Time	January 27	January 26	January 25
4th Sunday in Ordinary Time	February 3	— [20]	February 1
5th Sunday in Ordinary Time	February 10	February 9	February 8
6th Sunday in Ordinary Time	—	February 16	February 15
7th Sunday in Ordinary Time	—	February 23	—
8th Sunday in Ordinary Time	—	March 2	—
9th Sunday in Ordinary Time	—	—	—
Ash Wednesday	February 13	March 5	February 18
1st Sunday of Lent	February 17	March 9	February 22
2nd Sunday of Lent	February 24	March 16	March 1

19. The celebration of this Sunday is superceded by the Assumption.
20. The celebration of this Sunday is superceded by the feast of the Presentation of the Lord.

Sunday/Feast Day	2013 *(cont.)*	2014 *(cont.)*	2015 *(cont.)*
	Year C	*Year A*	*Year B*
3rd Sunday of Lent	March 3	March 23	March 8
4th Sunday of Lent	March 10	March 30	March 15
5th Sunday of Lent	March 17	April 6	March 22
Passion (Palm) Sunday	March 24	April 13	March 29
Holy Thursday	March 28	April 17	April 2
Good Friday	March 29	April 18	April 3
Easter Sunday	March 31	April 20	April 5
2nd Sunday of Easter	April 7	April 27	April 12
3rd Sunday of Easter	April 14	May 4	April 19
4th Sunday of Easter	April 21	May 11	April 26
5th Sunday of Easter	April 28	May 18	May 3
6th Sunday of Easter	May 5	May 25	May 10
Ascension	May 9	May 29	May 14
7th Sunday of Easter	May 12	June 1	May 17
Pentecost	May 19	June 8	May 24
Trinity Sunday	May 26	June 15	May 31
Body and Blood of Christ	June 2	June 22	June 7
9th Sunday in Ordinary Time	—	—	—
10th Sunday in Ordinary Time	June 9	—	June 14
11th Sunday in Ordinary Time	June 16	—	June 21
12th Sunday in Ordinary Time	June 23	—	June 28
13th Sunday in Ordinary Time	June 30	—[21]	July 5
14th Sunday in Ordinary Time	July 7	July 6	July 12
15th Sunday in Ordinary Time	July 14	July 13	July 19
16th Sunday in Ordinary Time	July 21	July 20	July 26
17th Sunday in Ordinary Time	July 28	July 27	August 2
18th Sunday in Ordinary Time	August 4	August 3	August 9
19th Sunday in Ordinary Time	August 11	August 10	August 16
20th Sunday in Ordinary Time	August 18	August 17	August 23
21st Sunday in Ordinary Time	August 25	August 24	August 30
22nd Sunday in Ordinary Time	September 1	August 31	September 6
23rd Sunday in Ordinary Time	September 8	September 7	September 13
24th Sunday in Ordinary Time	September 15	—[22]	September 20
25th Sunday in Ordinary Time	September 22	September 21	September 27
26th Sunday in Ordinary Time	September 29	September 28	October 4
27th Sunday in Ordinary Time	October 6	October 5	October 11
28th Sunday in Ordinary Time	October 13	October 12	October 18
29th Sunday in Ordinary Time	October 20	October 19	October 25
30th Sunday in Ordinary Time	October 27	October 26	—[25]
31st Sunday in Ordinary Time	November 3	—[23]	November 8
32nd Sunday in Ordinary Time	November 10	—[24]	November 15
33rd Sunday in Ordinary Time	November 17	November 16	November 22
Christ the King	November 24	November 23	November 29

21. The celebration of this Sunday is superceded by the feast of Peter and Paul, Apostles.
22. The celebration of this Sunday is superceded by the Triumph of the Cross.
23. The celebration of this Sunday is superceded by the feast of All Souls.
24. The celebration of this Sunday is superceded by the Dedication of St John Lateran.
25. The celebration of this Sunday is superceded by the feast of All Saints.

About the Authors

Eileen Drilling earned a BS in education from Mt. Mary College, Milwaukee, Wisconsin, and an MS in educational psychology and counseling from Winona State University, Winona, Minnesota. In the past Eileen taught elementary and junior high school, then worked as a faith formation coordinator. Ms. Drilling has written materials for the Hazelden Foundation.

Judy Rothfork earned a BA in education and English from Mt. Mary College in Milwaukee, Wisconsin, and an MA in education with an emphasis in guidance and counseling from the University of Colorado. She was an RCIA facilitator in California, where she was a member of the Diocese of Orange RCIA Catechetical Board. Judy has taught in Catholic elementary schools and coordinated faith formation programs.